T0333278

WATCH DOGS
LEGION

RESISTANCE REPORT

TITAN
BOOKS

London

An Insight Editions Book

PREFACE

Let me start with this: As a veteran journalist and concerned citizen of the world, I see no story of greater global significance than the one unfolding today in London. The city's brutal coupling of a privatized police regime with a cutthroat black-market economy, and a people's insurgency in response, is roiling the streets in a way that should strike fear into any modern democracy. This, first and foremost, is the urgent motive behind this work.

This report also explores the conflict's sociopolitical origins, placing London's turmoil in historical perspective. It reviews the rise of the modern authoritarian surveillance state—often referred to by the acronym MASS—and the emergence of a large, disparate region of opposition forces that's referred to collectively as the Resistance. In particular, I'll tunnel into the underground collective that has become the heart of antiauthoritarian resistance, not just in London but worldwide: the group that calls itself "DedSec."

As a credentialed reporter for several North American news agencies, I've pursued this larger story for nearly two decades. I've compiled a deep international roster of contacts in both communities—the Surveillance State and the Resistance—including many major players today in London, within both DedSec and UK intelligence circles. Any reports herein come from highly placed, confidential sources that, in some cases, I've cultivated for *decades*. Also note: *I do not reveal sources.* In many cases, such revelations would be lethal for both the source and, likely, me.

My point is, I've tried to make sense of the exigencies of the all-seeing, Hobbesian leviathan-state. In the past year, I've focused on its ominous emergence in London and profiled the counterforces arrayed against it.

But my personal, root interest in the topic—some might call it an obsession—began on a hot summer afternoon in 2003.

▼ ⧩ ▼

At 4:10 p.m. on August 14, 2003, I was prepping the oyster bar at Nelson's Cove, a seafood bistro in New York City's Greenwich Village. I'd shucked a tray of bluepoints and was arranging them on ice beds when the lights flickered and died. After a few minutes of darkness, I felt my way through tables toward the dim green glow of a battery-powered exit sign.

Outside on West Broadway, people were pouring out of darkened cafés and stores. It was a sweltering afternoon, jungle hot. Word spread fast that the entire city was powerless. A weird buzz—thrilling but distinctly threatening—vibrated in the street: *What's happening? Did they hit us again?*

Less than two years earlier, the twin towers had fallen just a few blocks to the south. The 9/11 scars were still fresh. This felt like a replay. Once again, a hundred thousand stranded commuters swarmed out of subway tunnels onto gridlocked streets to make the

long trek home across borough bridges. Some gave up and camped on the steps of the Central Post Office or other municipal buildings. Guys in suits curled up on sidewalks for the night.

That evening, in Albany, Governor Pataki declared a state of emergency and mobilized the National Guard. Amtrak's entire Northeast Corridor rail service failed, with all trains running into and out of New York City shut down. Area airports ceased operations. Circuit overloads disrupted cell phone service across the entire region. Wall Street and the United Nations went dark. Supermax prisons switched to generator power and went into emergency lockdown mode. State troopers deployed into stricken communities as forty thousand NYPD officers broke out their shields and military ordnance.

As on 9/11, in the name of public safety, civil liberties were suspended. Panicked authorities seized control of the streets, the airwaves, and the transportation grid—all for security's sake.

The Northeast Blackout of 2003 turned into the most widespread power outage in North American history. Fifty-five million people in eight states across the Northeast and upper Midwest regions were plunged into darkness for days—in some cases, weeks. The surge overload triggered the shutdown of nine nuclear reactors at power plants across New York, New Jersey, Ohio, and Michigan, stripping thousands more megawatts of electricity from the grid. All told, more than one hundred major power plants across the Northeast went completely offline.

What caused this catastrophe? The official story was hard to believe even then.

A special task force commissioned by Congress concluded that the limb of an overgrown tree in Walton Hills, Ohio, brushed against a single high-tension power line, triggering a series of system faults complicated by human error and software glitches.

My own extensive, eight-year investigation of the blackout confirmed that, indeed, the cascading faults—a sequence of twenty-six separate events—unfolded exactly as the task force reported. But years of digging through the tangled underground root system of antiauthoritarian hacktivism has led me to one key fact: The great blackout's initial trigger event was *not* a sagging tree branch in Ohio.

It was a guy in Chicago named T-Bone.

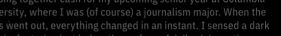

Today, most careful observers of London's turmoil know about Blume Corporation and its ctOS system, a fully integrated control and surveillance network. But back in 2003, Blume was a silent partner, operating under the radar with full lockdown control of the Northeast power grid.

That blackout in 2003, walking the edge of urban chaos, affected me in a deeply personal way. I'll never forget the feeling in the streets. Again, that's the gut-level reason why I'm writing this report.

I'd put in a lot of hard hours at the Village bistro that summer, scraping together cash for my upcoming senior year at Columbia University, where I was (of course) a journalism major. When the lights went out, everything changed in an instant. I sensed a dark anarchy festering just below the surface of daily civic routine.

I remember feeling twinges of both relief and fear at the sight of security checkpoints manned by cops in riot gear. I can't help but wonder how many Londoners must have felt the same when Albion's automated checkpoints began to spread throughout their city.

Civilization's thin veneer can melt away fast when food starts to spoil in your dead refrigerator while panic-buying empties shelves at every grocer in the tristate area. Sheer survival is a strong instinct, I've learned. It can be jarring to recognize how willing you can be to exchange your cherished freedoms for guaranteed food, safety, and comfort.

At times during the 2003 blackout, I found myself wondering: *Would a police state really be so bad for a while? Just until things settle down?*

That's how tyranny gets its foothold. I've seen it here in London, too. Like anywhere, the 6 o'clock news is riddled with sensationalist pieces on murder and crime. Lately the shaken bystanders interviewed always express the same thing: "Thank God Albion was here," they stutter out. "It could have been so much worse."

D: Remember what I told you at the Press Club banquet last month? Internal resistance at MI5 to their replacement by private Albion security—goons gone wild, deep institutional support, etc. Something bloody odd going on. Check out my weekly series for the national bureau this month. I'm calling it "Dispatches from Checkpoint London."

Better yet, come to London and have a gander. I've got people you need to meet. It might add an interesting chapter to that weighty tome you're writing.

Be careful, though. Don't let them tack an Optik ID implant behind your ear. They'll try, and honestly so many tourists chomp at the bit just for the chance to test it out. But you Yanks still get a free pass from Her Majesty's finest if you're willing to stand your ground in a small, secondary room in Heathrow. Though I'm sure you'll be flagged by Albion as a lower-tier person of interest for your trouble.

Cheers,

LH

METROPOL MISSING PERSONS REPORT:

NAME: LOUISE HARTFORD

OCCUPATION: SENIOR CORRESPONDENT, GBB INVESTIGATIONS UNIT

5'5", 8 STONE, 10 POUNDS

SLIM BUILD

DARK HAIR

WRIST TATTOO: BLUE ROSE

PART 1
ROOTS OF RAGE

This morning, working in my Lambeth hotel lobby, I witnessed the savage assault of a South Asian couple near the security checkpoint just outside.

The assailants were not street thugs. Their gear identified them as men from Albion, the private security force that has taken over most of the Metropolitan Police Service's duties. Nine months in London, and I fear what I'm seeing: The world is in danger of losing the great city that shrugged off the Blitz of 1940–1941.

Don't get me wrong—the *people* are not lost. The same cheeky, gritty British spirit of something that I'd term "belligerent survival" is alive and thriving in the streets today.

But I fear that the social glue that bonds all strata of society to a common civic purpose is steadily losing its grip.

▼△▼

One reason is that the enemy, such as it is, now dwells in the shadows.

Back in the darkest days of total war—when flocks of fat-winged German Heinkel 111s floated across the Channel to empty their bomb racks on London—the enemy was easy to identify. You could just point to the sky or to grainy news photos of Hitler and Göring huddled over their map of London in the Reich Ministry of Aviation.

As a result, Britain never wavered. Every citizen, from the king, prime minister, and members of Parliament on down to the constabulary, dockworker, and bricklayer—all huddled in air raid shelters and found a stunning common resolve.

Over the course of eight cruel months, London weathered thousands of Luftwaffe sorties, day and night, including seventy-one major "terror" raids that rained more than eighteen thousand tons of ordnance on civilian neighborhoods. The city never broke. Down in their dark holes, Londoners sang and even laughed as the ground shook.

Above them, Spitfires and Hurricanes scrambled into the air to engage the enemy.

▼△▼

But today, who is the enemy? Where is the enemy?

Today, we hear of horrors in Nine Elms, carnage in Camden. What's going on? Nobody seems to know. Disinformation is the new Gestapo.

Back in March 1941, the physics of a bomb's parabolic trajectory—inertia, airspeed, wind speed—could mean an entire family was obliterated in a single second. But today, something else is happening. Something far more insidious and frightening—and omnipresent—is tugging loose threads, one by one, from the city's fabric. Somebody is putting up checkpoints, ctOS drones, and cameras. And now they've put an Optik cranial implant in everyone's heads.

I fear London needs something more than Spitfires and Hurricanes to defend it this time.

THE GENESIS OF THE SURVEILLANCE STATE

HOW DID WE GET HERE?

Everyone knows the old adage popularized by President Theodore Roosevelt: "Speak softly and carry a big stick, you will go far." In the twenty-first century, however, the New World Order has found much more success with the carrot than the stick. The evolution of surveillance technologies and the creeping usurpation of privacy and freedom in recent decades was developed through an ever-expanding net of new technologies that began as small, unobtrusive advancements. Each shiny piece of state-of-the-art tech is sold to the public with the seductive promise of making things faster, easier, or more secure. The harsh reality we've had to face is that nothing is free. There's always, *always* someone on the other side of the screen, soaking up the data. And it's worth a lot of money.

In this section, I'll try to give a bit of a history lesson on how the fractured city of London, as I've come to know it the past nine months, came to exist.

CCTV

Ah, CCTV—what a natural start for any discussion about modern Great Britain. First used in Nazi Germany at top-secret V-2 missile sites during World War II, CCTV (closed-circuit television technology) began to spread relentlessly across the industrialized world after the war. Today, it's an increasingly omnipresent feature of modern life. But nowhere more so than London.

Today, centralized, government-run camera systems can track your movements from the moment you exit your home—and sometimes even before. London's Traffic and Environmental Zone employs hundreds of CCTV cameras, checkpoints, and barriers that track movement in the heart of the city, with a CCTV camera for every fourteen citizens, making Londoners the most surveilled population in the world. Recent studies estimate an installed base of more than 450 million CCTV cameras are now active worldwide, with millions more planned.

Watchdog groups like the American Civil Liberties Union (ACLU) have fought hard against the spread of CCTV public surveillance over the years. More recently, tech-savvy underground groups like DedSec have joined the fight against the steady erosion of privacy and the growing power of the corporate state.

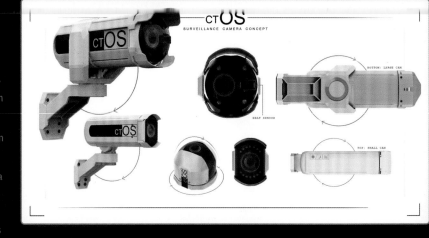

METADATA COLLECTION

After the trauma of the 9/11 attacks in the United States, the country's National Security Agency (NSA) undertook a massive counterterrorism effort, with a focus on electronic data gathering. A new program, authorized in 2006, began to collect and process all so-called "foreign intelligence" passing through American internet servers.

The program, code named PRISM, gained access to vast troves of private internet and telecommunication data from the user bases of the United States' largest technology companies—all designated as Special Source Operations (SSO).

Amazingly, PRISM's existence remained a secret until a full six years

evidence of the agency's activities, eventually revealing that PRISM collected an amount of private data that is the "the equivalent of one Library of Congress every 14.4 seconds." And while technically PRISM could not collect data on US citizens without a warrant, there were few ways for any oversight authority to confirm lawful compliance.

In the wake of Snowden's revelations, most Americans agreed that sacrificing civil liberties to such an extent for the sake of national security was unacceptable and outrageous. But that didn't stop PRISM, of course. In fact, the program became a model for state-sanctioned surveillance and bulk collection of data world-wide. If the NSA or CIA are experimenting with it, it's a damn safe bet that MI5 and their replacement will take a good look as well.

SIRS

I expect most Americans are already familiar with MI5, the United Kingdom's long-time domestic security and counterintelligence agency. The rise of MI5's successor, SIRS, however, warrants a good deal of explanation.

MI5's downfall and the birth of SIRS come down to cyberter-ror—though I can hardly write that word without thinking of that cheesy movie *Cyberdriver*. Regardless, over a period of weeks in 2018 and 2019, the city of Newcastle was crippled by a major cyberterror attack, with essential civic systems compromised for weeks. In response to the incident, the British intelligence agencies GCHQ (Government Communi-cations Headquarters) and MI5 assembled an antihacking task force that became colloqui-ally known as "Her Majesty's Snoops." They were popular, at first, but the group's overzeal-ous tactics quickly cost its political backing, and it nearly dissolved. Except . . .

That antihacking task force was reorganized to become the Signals Intelligence Response Service, or SIRS. The Service, as they like to call themselves, gobbled up MI5 in the reorganization. Technically, SIRS' charter directive is to interdict terrorism, both domestic and international; combat cybercrime; and infiltrate and dismantle organized crime firms in the UK. It's quite the platter of responsibilities, and you'd have to merge the FBI with the CIA to create an agency with a comparable mission in the United States.

Created by Parliament to counter twenty-first-century threats to national security, SIRS wields unlimited power to collect and analyze both public and private data with virtually no oversight, thanks to the 2016 Investigatory Powers Act. In a very short time, SIRS has grown to rival the NSA as the largest intelligence-gathering entity in the world. Rumors are that SIRS has tech so firmly under their belt that it puts PRISM to shame.

The question remains: What is SIRS doing with all their power and intel? As far as I can tell, one of SIRS' first assignments was to murder a suspect in the Newcastle incident. What a way to close the loop, am I right? Of course, the news reports say it's only a conspiracy theory, when they say anything at all.

ALBION

It's impossible to provide an adequate summary of SIRS without giving heed to Albion. This elite international contingent of ex-military, ex-police, and veteran soldiers of fortune is now widely considered the world's leading private military company (PMC). A favorite career haven for former Special Forces and dark ops intelligence operatives, Albion demands rigorous training in unconventional warfare techniques and modes of deployment, including counterterror and counterinsurgency tactics—particularly in urban settings.

Given this fearsome expertise—and the company director's extensive web of political contacts—it comes as no surprise that the UK government, in the wake of recent events, has expanded Albion's role into a more robust security presence throughout London. Since then, the company has engineered a de facto military occupation of the city, and Albion provides all public policing and private security issues.

An ongoing pro-Albion PR campaign continues to pander to those Londoners who fear the country is becoming lawless. But after months of brutal Albion thuggery directed at not only criminals—indiscriminate gunfights between organized crime street crews and Albion enforcers are common—but also legal public protests and demonstrations, London's residents now live in fear of becoming collateral damage.

FROM CELL PHONES TO OPTIK

More than a decade ago, American and British law enforcement agencies began taking advantage of new technology and outdated privacy laws to track and profile citizens with impunity. When powered on, a mobile phone registers its position with cell towers every few minutes, regardless of whether or not the device is being actively used. New GPS technologies thus allowed authorities to construct remarkably detailed "movement maps" of surveillance targets.

This tracking also reveals highly sensitive private behaviors: *Where did you spend the night? What stores did you visit? When did you see your psychologist? What political activities did you attend?*

Police or government intelligence agents can acquire this sort of personal information without even getting a warrant from a judge. But in an extreme counterterror environment, it gets much worse. Today, in London, contract security personnel are far less bound by legal restraints—in part because the technology landscape has evolved.

Nobody in London—or rather, *almost* nobody—carries a smartphone anymore. Instead, there's the Optik Device. While I do cover much of the new tech deployed by SIRS, Albion, and the Resistance in Part 5, you'll need to understand the ubiquitous Optik if you hope to navigate the labyrinthine forces coalescing in London, so I'll debrief here.

THE WORLD'S FINEST FOR ENGLAND

ALBION
PRIVATE SERVICES

SIGNING BONUS AND CITIZENSHIP SPONSORSHIP FOR IMMIGRANT APPLICANTS.

OPTIK

OPTIK 1.0: GEEKY!

Funny how fashion works. When Blume released the original Optik, a much-hyped wearable smartphone AR (augmented reality) accessory, it was widely ridiculed for being a years-late rehash of old glasses-frame-based ideas. Nobody bought them. It was an out-and-out disaster for Blume and panned in the press. Then, out of nowhere (I'm guessing some virtual envelopes of e-cash were involved), the London Transit Commission discontinued the Oyster travel card program and made the Optik device the *only* way to pay for your Tube fare. Touted as a convenience/security measure, this new system had the less publicized effect of total movement tracking for anyone passing through the Underground system.

Last year, however, Blume launched Optik 2.0. Today, everyone just calls it Optik—which speaks to just how little of a blip the 1.0 version made. Unlike the old glasses-based design, Optik 2.0 was touted by Blume as the first personal device with a truly integrated augmented reality (AR) experience. The trick is, it's all made possible via a cranial implant. Basically . . . they put a chip in your skull. But hey, anything not to wear those hideous glasses, right?

Don't worry, though, it's not *that* invasive. A small post is implanted just in front of the ear in a nonsurgical procedure about as involved as an ear piercing. The crown jewel of Blume's R&D division, the device is capable of bombarding your optical nerve with electrical signals, making it possible to hijack how your brain interprets what you see—and thus allowing the device to render graphics directly to your vision.

Billed as a revolutionary step forward in h "brain/reality interface," these personal r what is called *enhanced imaging vision.* N the city's central operating system, the Op overlays that map locations and identify o readouts directly onto the wearer's field o (heads-up display).

It's important to note that the Optik's mai device attached to the implanted post ove dymium magnet. The external Optik itself upgrades or vanity models. Some naive us the external unit grants them temporary p

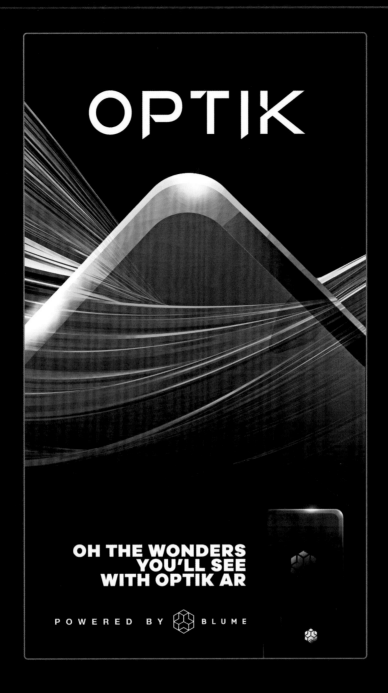

**OH THE WONDERS
YOU'LL SEE
WITH OPTIK AR**

POWERED BY BLUME

OPTIK ADOPTION

Despite the need for a semipermanent dermal implant, the Optik debuted to incredible popularity, confounding analysts everywhere. The efficiencies and conveniences of the HUD proved too enticing to Londoners, helped along by a massive marketing push by Blume. Now, the Optik is mandatory for all London citizens as the primary form of identification. Anyone found without one is subject to fines or arrest.

How is it all paid for? Well, the Optik is given away for free in exchange for Blume's ISP monopoly. (What a bargain!) All other providers are locked out. The Optik device runs on the new ctOS implementation in London, employing an autonomous load-balancing, drone-based wireless network. Traditional cellular

networks were no longer supported by government grants and funding, so they were phased out, along with the traditional smartphones that rely on them.

So, while most of London opted in to life with an Optik ID implant, the rest were dragged into the mess through legislation. The situation has created as ripe an opportunity for the surveillance state as could be imagined. Even in Optik's so-called Privacy Mode, ctOS still collects its baseline of metadata. That means it knows where people go, who they visit, what they see and buy and eat, when they sleep and wake and exercise—everything just short of reading actual thoughts and feelings. Actually, scratch that. Machine learning has just about solved how to discern thoughts and feelings from the digital footprint, hasn't it?

FACIAL RECOGNITION

Facial recognition ("face rec") biometry may be the most insidiously invasive ID tool ever deployed for public surveillance purposes. Unlike other biometrics such as DNA or fingerprints, face rec doesn't require consent, knowledge, or even participation of the subject. Thanks to the vast database of high-definition images created via government photo ID requirements, these days it's nearly impossible to move through any public space (and many private spaces too) without being recognized and logged in real time.

In London, more than 250,000 fixed or drone-mounted Blume 4K Ultra HD CCTV public surveillance cameras with night-vision and infrared scanners keep an eye on every nook and cranny of the city, high and low, day and night. Every camera feed is run through a ctOS facial scan platform, giving the authorities, corporations, and even certain individuals a real-time motion map, tracking every citizen's every move.

Every day, UK law enforcement authorities add new data to their vast and growing cache of population biometrics. Private companies are jumping in, too. Social media sites have been developing facial recognition databases for years. We have no idea how these private biometric datasets are being used, aggregated, or sold. But certainly, one goal is to allow every security operative, public or private, to instantaneously ID any individual encountered.

GBB NEWS

Security Drone Thwarts Brazen Grocery Grab, Armed Drifter Killed in South Bank Robbery

In a brilliant bit of ironic justice, a deranged gunman was torn to fleshy shreds by an Albion police drone after trying to shoot an automated shelf-stocker robot during a wild robbery attempt at a South Bank grocer on Sunday.

Amaichi Davis, 41, entered the Highpoint Foods supermarket on Waterloo Road just after noon and asked to speak with the store manager. Witnesses reported hearing sounds of breaking glass and loud shouting, followed shortly by a burst of semiautomatic gunfire. A team of Albion first responders arrived minutes later to secure the site.

"Our initial investigation indicates that Mr. Davis was an antigovernment radical with a history of violence," said Albion PMC spokesman Earl Harrington at a press briefing just hours after the incident. "Our security team made a concerted attempt to defuse the situation peacefully, but to no avail."

Not even remotely what it seems. Check it out! —Louise

Flying about ten meters above the surface roads of London is an AI-directed drone ecosystem that has become absolutely omnipresent. I confess after my first few weeks here, I found, to my chagrin, that I hardly noticed them anymore.

The drone highway first took aim at disrupting package delivery, resulting in faster transportation of goods and—to the cheers of commuters across the greater London metro area—reduced congestion on the roads, all with the added benefit of lowering greenhouse gas emissions. Today, drones deliver food, medicines, and other goods; administer repairs; aid in construction; . . . you name it, they've either got a drone for it or I can assure you Blume Corporation or the adorably branded start-up Parcel Fox are working on one.

Drone traffic is a highly regulated industry. The UK passed sweeping drone legislation that essentially outlaws personal drones while establishing a complex set of regulations governing the deployment of commercial or industrial drones in high-density spaces. It's worth noting that rapid interregional commercial drone traffic is strictly assigned to high-altitude lanes; the local drone traffic drifting above city streets is restricted to slower-paced duties.

Given their pervasiveness, it was only a matter of time before drones became an important part of London's law enforcement efforts. While early CCTV surveillance was based on networks of cameras installed in fixed locations—on buildings, bridge spans, traffic signals, and other public structures—society's latest beloved tech has resulted in a new class of video surveillance: the spy drone network.

Equipped with advanced video cameras, infrared sensors, and lock-on pursuit capabilities, drones in distributed networks enable mass tracking of people and vehicles over wide areas both exterior and interior, no matter how chaotic or congested. Micro-drones can hover over a walled private yard or peer into windows of a home or office.

Despite furious public and legislative debate, law enforcement agencies have significantly expanded their use of drone surveillance, particularly in dense urban environments like London as a response to the rising crime in cities. Today, a UK citizen's every move can be monitored, tracked, recorded, and analyzed by an AI-directed drone network. Drones equipped with weapons (both nonlethal and lethal) also assist in crowd control and suspect roundup activities.

IF I DON'T KNOW YOU I DON'T TRUST YOU

SECURELONDON

IF YOU SEE OR HEAR ANY SUSPICIOUS BEHAVIOR OR
UNATTENDED PACKAGES, FOR LONDON'S SAKE
REPORT IT TO THE AUTHORITIES.

SIGNAL
INTELLIGENCE
RESPONSE
SERVICE SIRS

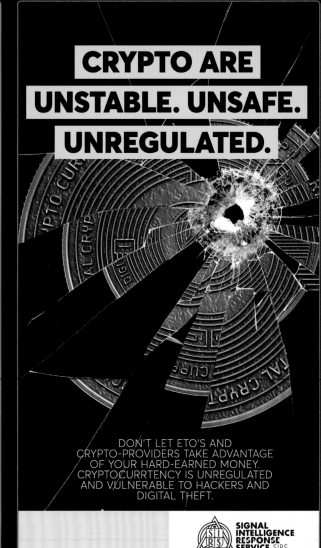

CRYPTO ARE UNSTABLE. UNSAFE. UNREGULATED.

DON'T LET ETO'S AND
CRYPTO-PROVIDERS TAKE ADVANTAGE
OF YOUR HARD-EARNED MONEY.
CRYPTOCURRTENCY IS UNREGULATED
AND VULNERABLE TO HACKERS AND
DIGITAL THEFT.

SIGNAL
INTELLIGENCE
RESPONSE
SERVICE SIRS

The power vacuum has created an opening for homegrown criminal talent to rise to influence in a way not seen since the Krays. Whether by their cruelty or their forward thinking in terms of embracing the dark web and cryptocurrency schemes, one family-run operation in particular has taken a meteoric rise: Clan Kelley.

Today, Clan Kelley maintains a controlling interest in London's booming underground economy, giving it the leverage necessary to lock down control of the city's black market. Any foreign cybercriminals wanting to do business in London now have the Kelleys as a gatekeeper.

THE EARLY RESISTANCE

Many modern underground antiauthoritarian movements can trace their origins and inspiration to the French Resistance that took place from 1940 to 1944. Operating under the boot of Nazi occupation, hundreds of small sleeper cells coordinated to conduct guerilla warfare, collect firsthand military intelligence for Allied forces, and maintain critical information pipelines to communities across France.

Today, resistance to neofascist tyranny must mobilize on two fronts operating in a coordinated fashion. Certainly, every popular uprising starts with active resistance deployment—that is, a deep pool of committed, passionate members willing to flood the streets and put their bodies on the line. But control of the cyber-scape is equally important. Given the internet's reach and power, any successful resistance movement must include a robust cyber-ops component. Technology has become so accessible and direct, and such an integral part of our lives that even those with zero coding abilities now possess the tools to fight back.

Thus, we are now seeing the rebirth of the DedSec—what used to be a hacktivist collective has transformed into a full-fledged, multi-level resistance movement in London with hackers, street fighters, and everything in between. All of this has roots reaching down into the recent past.

ACTIVE RESISTANCE

In the United Kingdom, active resistance groups have confronted far-right movements consistently over the years—for example, the fascist, racist, anti-Semitic National Front (NF) of the 1970s. Founded in 1967, the Front fanned xenophobic fears of South Asian migration to build a loyal following that translated into local electoral gains, using rallies and street marches to attract new members.

But by 1974, once-timid protesters had begun to organize and initiate active resistance tactics in opposition to the ultra-authoritarian Front. That year, in a series of events known as the Red Lion Square disorders, a scheduled NF march ended up in a tense face-off with counterdemonstrators. Then, in August 1977, a violent clash dubbed the Battle of Lewisham pitted another neo-Nazi column of National Front marchers against a huge coalition of antifascist activist groups more than 4,000 strong. The overwhelming response helped trigger the decline of the National Front as a relevant force in British culture and politics.

In the United States, the massive civil rights and antiwar movements of the 1950s and '60s formed a solid core of active resistance political activism. Later, the Anti-Racist Action Network (ARA), founded in 1987, became a bulwark of antifascism, disrupting the local and nationwide activities of neo-Nazi and white supremacist groups. It became the precursor to the antiauthoritarian movements active today.

As the ever-watchful eye of ctOS and Albion security forces continue to transform London, the city finds itself on a precipice as resistance forces begin to organize in opposition to these authoritarian forces.

CYBERRESISTANCE: A BRIEF HISTORY OF HACKTIVISM

No simple narrative can truly encompass the history of such a protean, quicksilver force as "hacktivism." Much of that history is shrouded in lore, legend, and outright disinformation, often by careful design. That's just the nature of hacker culture.

The term itself, first coined in 1992, combines the terms "hacker" and "activism." And yes, it is true that hacktivists tend to be hackers with a political or social agenda. But those agendas are fluid, tailored to individual idiosyncrasy, and not without certain outright antisocial aspects.

Indeed, the root term "hacker" can refer to anyone with technical skills, but it more typically indicates someone who uses exceptional computer skills to gain unauthorized access to heavily protected systems or networks. The purpose of hacking can be almost anything—to steal money, plant lighthearted messages, commit blackmail, troll pompous celebrities, or any number of other motivations.

But a "hacktivist" is said to have a higher cause, even a mission—to expose nasty military secrets, challenge corporate greed or the corrupt machinations of government, fight internet censorship and control, exploit security flaws as a public service, or achieve other political goals. Hacktivism has been described as "the transposition of demonstrations, civil disobedience, and low-level information warfare into cyberspace."

Many hacktivist "hives" have gained fame (or infamy) over the past thirty years, and I hate to give any of them short shrift because . . . well, frankly, I'm afraid of them. But there's one group I'm obligated to discuss at length: DedSec.

DEDSEC AND ctOS

Originally, DedSec engaged in relatively low-level, innocuous hacks that were more symbolic than anything. Consisting primarily of software engineers formerly employed at Umeni—a CIA contractor and private military company that specialized in cryptography, cybersecurity and metadata intelligence collection—the group created a loose leadership referred to as the "Council of Daves" and dedicated itself to a generalized fight against corporate greed and corruption.

But in 2011, Blume Corporation completed final QA testing on a remarkably powerful, AI-controlled central operating system called ctOS. Chicago became the first major urban center to implement ctOS citywide, placing its entire infrastructure—utilities, traffic control, public transit, bridges and tunnels, telecom, and much more—in the hands of a centralized computer system. The effects were felt overnight. Traffic and commute times plummeted. Police, fire, and ambulance response times improved exponentially, and emergency room wait times were halved. The weeks that followed revealed other, less obvious but just as spectacular, improvements to the city government's bottom line, with the move to ctOS correlating with massive admin and energy savings.

ctOS adoption wasn't meant to make the city only more efficient, but also safer. The core monitoring system was linked to a mass surveillance network, making Chicago the first "Big Brother" city. If a known criminal so much as sneezed, ctOS was ready to dispatch the authorities. Much more insidious, ctOS also included a highly controversial Crime Prediction System that used facial and pattern recognition as well as action-prediction algorithms to spot potential criminals and victims. All this power in the hands of a single corporation. What, you might wonder, could go wrong?

As details of the ctOS deployment were unveiled, DedSec quickly agreed on a new overriding mission: to disable and discredit this cyber-behemoth. DedSec ops began to focus on attacking various ctOS systems to reveal their vulnerabilities . . . and more importantly, their frightening Big Brother capabilities.

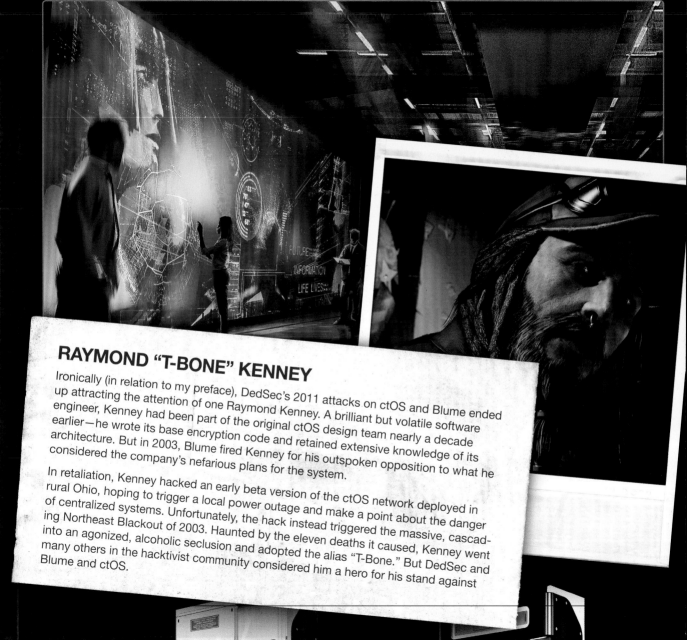

RAYMOND "T-BONE" KENNEY

Ironically (in relation to my preface), DedSec's 2011 attacks on ctOS and Blume ended up attracting the attention of one Raymond Kenney. A brilliant but volatile software engineer, Kenney had been part of the original ctOS design team nearly a decade earlier—he wrote its base encryption code and retained extensive knowledge of its architecture. But in 2003, Blume fired Kenney for his outspoken opposition to what he considered the company's nefarious plans for the system.

In retaliation, Kenney hacked an early beta version of the ctOS network deployed in rural Ohio, hoping to trigger a local power outage and make a point about the danger of centralized systems. Unfortunately, the hack instead triggered the massive, cascading Northeast Blackout of 2003. Haunted by the eleven deaths it caused, Kenney went into an agonized, alcoholic seclusion and adopted the alias "T-Bone." But DedSec and many others in the hacktivist community considered him a hero for his stand against Blume and ctOS.

In 2014, despite the Chicago outcome, Blume Corporation finished development of ctOS 2.0. The sophisticated upgrade, said to "connect everyone with everything," was implemented in the San Francisco Bay Area, Dublin, Dubai, and Seoul. The Bay Area rollout drew the immediate attention of the active DedSec cell in the city, which began to target the system. This San Francisco team eventually discovered how stolen data harvested via ctOS was being manipulated to leverage global financial markets. The exposed scheme took down Blume's CTO and mastermind of the plot, Dušan Nemec.

But despite the ensuing investigation of the company, Blume continued its ctOS development cycle unabated, beginning its roll-out of ctOS in Europe via a long-term plan that began in London. The ambitious strategy was spearheaded, almost innocuously, by a scheme to eventually replace the city's CCTV network with cameras connected to Blume's ctOS cloud. Blume initially focused on the private sector, approaching small business owners throughout London, to offer deeply discounted (or free, when that's what it took to get the release forms signed and their hardware installed) CCTV hardware, gradually building a deep infrastructure of ctOS-compatible cameras throughout the city.

As Blume gained traction in London, the company approached the City of London mayor's office with a bold proposition. Blume would work with local government to convert all CCTV systems in London to run on central, Blume-controlled servers. This would give government agencies new analysis capabilities, leveraging Blume's cutting-edge new machine-learning and image-recognition systems. In return, Blume would receive massive government subsidies and assistance. The most visible symbol of this devil's bargain looms over Fitzrovia, where Blume has converted the famous '60's-era eyesore into their London corporate headquarters, drone hive, and central AI processing center.

Once Blume occupied the tower, the rest came quickly. Civic regulations paved the way for a comprehensive ctOS drone surveillance network, existing data providers were shouldered out of business, and Blume debuted their Optik device—robust tracking and data collection technology disguised as a next-gen replacement for consumer smartphone devices.

Today, thanks to all of this, London is the most watched city in the world. Londoners' every move is tracked, whether by cameras, via their digital shadow on ctOS, or simply by tracking their physical location 24/7 via their implanted Optik.

And DedSec finds itself in the belly of the Hobbesian beast.

They're surveilling you too, mate.

I've learned a way to deactivate my implant
for short blips. I'll stop by your room later.
Let's catch up, shall we?

* LOUISE — GOOSE GARDEN BISTRO, MARCH 9

* 2 MONTHS BEFORE DISAPPEARANCE

CHECKPOINT LONDON

Tonight, a National Front anti-immigrant rally in Brockwell Park—not far from my hotel on Half Moon Lane—turned into a nasty, rock-tossing mob.

I was returning from dinner with a few colleagues, all journalists based in London. Despite wading through the toxic swamp of US political culture in recent years, I was shocked to hear an MP recently refer to the London press corps as "treasonous vermin infesting Her Majesty's Government."

During the meal, my friends all joked about their new status as enemies of the state. But one of them, a well-known investigative reporter for the GBB, admitted she was beginning to fear for her safety. Every day, she said, thugs lurked across the street from her office, staring up at her window. She got vile, threatening notes in her inbox.

"I'm convinced my Optik doesn't like me, either," she said, laughing as she tapped a spot just in front of her right ear.

She spoke lightly, but her look told me something else. Then she slid me a note that read: *They're surveilling you too, mate.*

Afterward, my cabby had to take a crazy, serpentine route around the Brockwell Park rally to get me safely back to my hotel entrance. En route, I caught sight of protestors on the fringes of the massive crowd. Something about their movements—the threatening, kinetic nature of their energy—really gave me a chill.

These were truly angry people.

Look, I'm just a Yank, and I don't claim any special insight into the zeitgeist of this city. But rage is not something that I typically associate with British culture. I've visited London enough times over the years to recognize a marked change in tone—a distinctly dark, angry turn for the worse.

Rage is the new medium. People are mad at immigrants, who they conflate with "job-stealing terrorists," as if that made any sense whatsoever. They're mad at the government. They're mad at elites—financial, academic, entertainment, media. In fact, it seems the only person they're *not* mad at is the Queen. Although the rest of the Royal Family can sod off.

More and more, *everyone* is afraid. Meanwhile, Big Brother is watching everything.

SURVEY OF KEY EVENTS

Before delving further into the current state of affairs, it's important to review how London got to where it is now. Here's a look at a string of select events that led to the city's catastrophic meltdown of civil liberties.

POLITICS

THE SUN SETS ON THE UNITED KINGDOM

It all started with the B word, or Brexit, and the less said about that the better. Let's jus say that from 2016 on, when departure wa finalized, the tightly woven fabric of the UK started unraveling.

 ### SCOTLAND SEPARATES

Holyrood, the Scottish capital, gave Westmin ster the vicky with a successful referendum vote to leave the United Kingdom. The UK flag was changed to reflect the independenc of Scotland and to better represent Wales, removing the blue field for St. Andrew's Cros and adding the black field and gold trim of the St. David's Cross. The new UK flag is now mockingly referred to as the "Black Jack."

IRISH DISCORD

At present, Northern Ireland maintains its position within the United Kingdom, though some people campaign for unification with the Republic. Multiple members of Ireland' Sinn Féin political party have been brought down by various political and personal scandals exposed by the published hacks their personal emails. Whispers of sabotag from within were rampant, but the hacks were never formally investigated.

PM HASSANI

Recently, Prime Minister Dev Hassani has been on yet another one of his diplomatic visits across the globe. Local reporters hav referred to this extended trip as "Hassani's Holiday," implying that he's actively avoid- ing time within the UK as a way to distance himself from the volatile state of domestic politics. And can you blame him?

Some Londoners clearly can – Hassani has become a symbol of all the ineffectual, centrist bureaucrats who have risen to power in recent years. Protesters frequently gather outside of an often-vacant 10 Downing stree to express their frustration with government officials who seem unwilling or unable to ste the tides of chaos overtaking London.

ECONOMY

RISE OF CRYPTO

The pound dropped by 10 percent and the Bank of England officially declared a recession. Confidence in the pound sterling eroded as the E-Token (or ETO) cryptocurrency—used at this point by tens of thousands of UK residents in peer-to-peer transactions—became increasingly stable. The public perception of "crypto" shifted, and ETO moved toward the mainstream.

E-Token vendors, particularly Quanta Bank, began offering very quick and inexpensive conversion from pounds to Bitcoin. They suddenly found themselves among the richest financial services companies in London.

When you've got a lot of cash, why not put out the flash? Recently, Quanta Bank installed dozens of E-Token cash machines across London neighborhoods. Parliament tried to stop them, but recanted after significant public backlash.

Cryptocurrency is now a flashpoint in UK politics; a sharp divide is drawn between those who see the ETO currency as an affordable, stable alternative to the unstable pound and those who consider it unpatriotic to use ETO, which is widely seen as undermining the British economy.

SPECIAL ECONOMIC ZONE

Attempting to have their financial Victoria sponge and eat it, too, London was declared a "Special Economic Zone." From here, the government thought they would curry favor with European governments and broker new trade agreements and private business deals intended to maintain the prominence of the UK financial sector. Results have been mixed, given that some European governments have a bit of an issue dealing with a police—sorry—Albion state.

LOCAL ECONOMY HITS THE BOTTOM AND KEEPS DIGGING

Within a few years, the British economy has descended from "slowing" to "recession" to full-on "depression." The Bank of England refuses to acknowledge the crisis fully, however, perhaps hoping to keep up appearances despite the writing on the wall.

MASS UNEMPLOYMENT CRISIS

Sweeping austerity measures led to thirteen thousand public employees being laid off over a matter of months. This sparked violent protests for a minimum guaranteed income, which became known as "Redundant Friday." While most countries in this moment considered a universal basic income a pie-in-the-sky dream, considering that unemployment has reached its highest levels since before World War II (you know, during that *other* depression), those idealists may have a point.

STATE OF SURVEILLANCE

CTOS CROSSES THE POND

Blume Corporation rolled out ctOS Europe, a brash (and wildly successful) plan that began in London. It included a multibillion-pound deal to replace all of the city's CCTV networks with improved cameras. These cameras connect to Blume's cloud and leverage their machine learning and image recognition systems. Within a year, 65 percent of cameras belonging to the city were replaced, and more than 80 percent of private cameras were on the ctOS system. Keeping an eye on Londoners has never been more efficient.

BLUME'S LONDON EXPANSION

Blume purchased the BT Tower and announced the coming deployment of their new BroadWave high-speed service aimed (initially) at enterprise licenses and ultrawealthy private citizens. The project was widely criticized as elitist, and the new look of the BT Tower was (and still is) ridiculed.

If only the building was their biggest ambition . . .

BLUME DATA MONOPOLY

In the interest of preventing "cybercrime" (to use the dated expression), a so-called Snoopers' Charter was passed, then passed again with even stricter requirements. At this point, all encrypted email/messaging services have been declared illegal in the UK. Blume struck a deal to become the exclusive ISP of the UK, promising to respect the Snoopers' Charter 2.0 laws and pushing updates to their devices to block encrypted messaging services.

IMMIGRATION ISOLATION

Following the B-word shitshow, xenophobes got their way and Parliament set a date by which all undocumented residents had to vacate the United Kingdom. Proimmigrant protests broke out, followed by larger "Kick Them Out" protests.

One highly publicized deportation case of a Romanian doctor and his family caught the public's attention and became a divisive media

story. Rumors of a jackbooted deportation force spread throughout the Internet, setting off a panic among undocumented residents. There was a sudden exodus, overwhelming the airports and trains. Some demanded to be considered refugees.

Perhaps as notable as the story itself is the fact that this story was one of the last such reported widely within Britain.

DEPORTEE CRISIS

REFUGEES REFUSED

UK immigration officials faced an unexpected hurdle when the EU began refusing to process deportation claims arriving by land. Instead, the EU asserted, these cases needed to be settled on British soil, before arriving in Europe. A temporary emigration office was set up in Southwark as a gesture of goodwill, but it was quickly overwhelmed, and a satellite office was opened in Hackney. Families trapped in immigration limbo began camping in the streets near both facilities.

KENNINGTON OVAL CAMP

A few months later, still struggling to cope with a swelling population of migrants (who both the UK and EU refused to acknowledge as refugees), the Elek Cricket Grounds at Kennington Oval was put under temporary lease. The move sparked public rage among those who saw the co-opting of a cricket ground as an affront to UK cultural identity.

Despite an early media blitz touting the relief resources and state-of-the-art temporary structures erected within, the cricket grounds soon became a fetid swamp of a refugee camp. All semblance of a humane operation vanished when a cooking fire got out of control and partially destroyed the exterior wall (funny how the media didn't cover any casualties, or why local fire brigades failed to respond until the fire was lighting the Vauxhall night sky).

A couple of months later (according to my sources), organized crime syndicate Clan Kelley hacked the Elek grounds registration files, gaining access to the personal case information of every person processed there. Apparently, the powers that be haven't noticed yet, or don't care, because Clan Kelley is now specifically targeting the most desperate refugees to exploit and recruit into their own service. For them, the Oval is a perpetual giving tree of cheap labor.

A few months ago, an Australian journalist went undercover in Kennington Oval for two weeks, then published an explosive exposé on the deplorable conditions within. The story was quickly picked up by news agencies worldwide. The political class was pressured to slow its deportation efforts . . . not that they're closing the Oval.

Oh, and if life wasn't shitty enough for the migrants inside, the English Patriotic Action Front (EPAF) is currently occupying the camp.

TOAN

Brainchild of futurist wunderkind Skye Larsen, the "Technology of All Nations" global conference, also known as TOAN, was touted as a new world's fair for technology. Larsen was supposed to give the keynote address, entitled "Super Intelligent AI Problem Solving." Hoping to demonstrate London's continued relevance, the UK spent millions to bring financial and techno-elites from all over the world. The press aptly nicknamed the conference "TOAN Deaf," lampooning the conference's over-the-top and out-of-touch marketing efforts. Supposedly a venue to discuss innovative new solutions to the pressing issues of the day—the housing crisis, the wealth gap, and the collapsing economy for starters—the conference seemed destined to devolve into a chance for the super-rich to mingle and network.

Then tragedy struck. On the first full day of the TOAN conference, a bomb went off, destroying the building and part of Blackfriar's bridge. The devastating attack killed dozens, though keynote speaker Skye Larsen survived—she was delivering her speech via hologram. Though no one took credit for the bombing, the media put the blame on "foreign terrorists," which helped stoke anti-immigrant sentiment in the city.

The same night featured a simultaneous bombing attack attempted against Parliament. Albion, personally led by their CEO Nigel Cass on-site, thwarted the attempt and the alleged bomber was killed in the altercation. Albion's star was immediately on the rise. Claiming that they needed better access to the city to prevent further attacks, Albion was quickly granted unfettered control of the streets, and set up dozens of new checkpoints throughout London.

GLOBAL BRITISH BROADCASTING (GBB)

Yes, our favorite source of costume dramas and Shakespearean actors with splendid accents has been privatized, sold to an unnamed group of foreign investors. But even better, leaked documents show that the GBB is now taking editorial instruction from SIRS. The story's gotten out to international outlets, but to my absolute lack of surprise, few locals have any idea.

ASSESSMENT: THE CURRENT STATE OF AFFAIRS

Not a pretty picture, is it? The great city of London, long a crown jewel of Western civilization, is tearing itself apart. Dark forces are trying to normalize dark impulses. A new status quo based on xenophobia, population control, intrusive surveillance, and pressure to "conform and inform" is sweeping the kingdom: *Keep an eye on your neighbor. Be a rat. Protect the purity of the homeland.*

Yes, London is at war with itself, and the current situation grows increasingly dire.

A STICKY POLITICAL WICKET

The Brexit mess feels like a distant memory, but it leaves a long, long shadow. When Scotland voted to leave the UK and join the EU as an independent nation, the change was reflected in the design of the new "Black Jack" flag. Ironically, the traditional Union Jack became a politically-charged symbol of defiance, often featured in Resistance artwork that thumbs its nose at the status quo, or worn on vintage T-shirts by cheeky teenagers hoping piss off their conservative parents.

Meanwhile, the UK's socioeconomic tailspin in Brexit's wake has spawned a virulent new strain of racist, ultranationalist politics and antiglobal isolationism. Political opportunists exploiting years of paranoid populist rhetoric and Internet agitprop have fallen back on an age-old tactic: Scapegoat "outsiders" (immigrants) and stoke fear. The goal: a new security state, amassing influence over the financial, technology, and intelligence sectors that drive daily life in the city.

Prime Minister Dev Hassani has proven to be a remarkably weak bureaucrat, easily manipulated by power brokers savvier in the ways of realpolitik. Hassani has, in effect, fled London via a series of extended "diplomatic visits" abroad. Democracy in the UK has been reduced to political theater—most members of Parliament are incompetent, ineffective, or compromised.

The Queen is notably absent from public view, leading to concerns about her health and whereabouts. The royal family remains tight-lipped on current affairs and generally withdrawn from media and other appearances.

Meanwhile, the UK's military has been embroiled in a series of unpopular foreign wars over the past decade that not only drain the public coffers but increase the need for private security companies—like Albion—to help keep the peace on the home front.

spiking at a near hundred-year high, dating back to the Great Depression of the 1930s. Britain's middle class is evaporating, and thousands are jobless across the city, blue and white collars alike. As a result, the population of rough sleepers is swelling.

British workplace. Blue-collar industrial and tech-sector jobs have been automated at an astounding rate, eliminating many of them as "redundant."

This troubling dynamic is breeding resentment in workers at every level of the economy as unemployment rapidly spreads. National frustrations came to a head a few years back during the bloody "Redundancy Riots" when an antitech rally on Trafalgar Square turned violent—thanks in no small part to Albion's heavy-handed-

With austerity measures starving public programs of funding, grassroots and nonprofit organizations have struggled to provide a safety net for the waves of unemployed. Churches offer public services, doctors and nurses provide care on the street, and paralegals assist those at risk of deportation with their case files,

THE IMMIGRATION "CRISIS"

With immigrant deportation sold as a political solution to an angry, suffering working class, the UK government has opened Repatriation Processing Centers (essentially, mass internment camps) to manage the flood of people identified and detained by SIRS as "illegals." Hunted down daily by relentless deportation squads, nonnatives are being shuttled into emigration facilities already overwhelmed with refugees.

The EU, in response to Britain's aggressive enforcement of its immigration laws, has put a freeze on processing the UK's deportees. As a result, the internment camps (sorry, "emigration centres") are growing to unmanageable sizes. The largest of these is Kennington Oval—known simply as "the Oval"—a converted cricket ground that has become a hellish detention center where desperate people scheduled for deportation are forced to await case reviews that may be months or years off.

Worst of all, sources report that both Albion private security and Clan Kelley, the organized crime firm, have turned this perverse situation to their advantage in remarkably similar ways, exploiting those made most vulnerable. Even fully naturalized citizens of immigrant descent, if seen as promising Albion recruits, are often flagged for deportation, and then they are offered leniency and work permits—but only if they sign on for stints with Albion capture squads. This feeds a grim circle, as newly minted Albion recruits often find themselves reluctantly targeting people with very similar stories to themselves.

Meanwhile, Clan Kelley makes highly exploitive offers of employment to desperate deportees with promises of forged paperwork and payment in untraceable cryptocurrency. These bargains are always worse than they seem. Hundreds of people find themselves trapped in modern forms of indentured servitude, totally subject to the whims of their criminal overseers.

Huge swaths of London's population live in fear of these two groups and their tactics, yet they have almost nowhere to turn for help.

INTERVIEW NOTES: 8/22

Dispatches from Checkpoint London

Met subject KS at 8:30 p.m. in Foyles bookstore and café, Charing Cross Road. Said he felt protected there "surrounded by two hundred thousand books."

Position: Level LE-04 Emigration Registry Clerk, Kennington Oval Processing Center

Full transcript included, but begin dispatch with following exchange:

LOUISE HARTFORD: *Your message said you'd seen "bad things." Can you be specific?*

KS: People are disappearing from the camps.

LH: Escaping?

KS: No. [*nervous*] I mean, at first I assumed they were escaping, just running back into the city. But that's not it, not at all.

LH: What's happening?

KS: Somebody's *buying* people, Ms. Hartford. Like livestock. Worse than livestock, really . . .

LH: Who?

KS: The Kelley people, for one. It's, you know . . . it's very hard to describe. The illegals, they're being sold, chipped, and tracked.

LH: Isn't everyone chipped and tracked these days?

KS: The Kelley implant is different.

LH: How so?

KS: [*nervous silence*]

LH: How do you know all this?

KS: My registry supervisor is conducting transactions. [*with revulsion*] Look, I've seen the implant, how it works.

LH: So what's happening to these people?

KS: Slaves, some of them. Others, I've heard, it's medical purposes.

LH: Medical?

KS: [*nervous glance around*] Let yourself imagine the worst possible interpretation of that word, Ms. Hartford.

COUNTERTERROR & CIVIL LIBERTIES

A few years back, manifestations of civil unrest like the Redundancy Riots, the Newcastle Incident, and the far-right Peckham Protest were shaking Britain's polite society to its very core. Deep-seated (and quite understandable) fears of terror attacks like the 7/7 bombings of 2005, the 2017 attacks on London Bridge and Manchester Arena, and the recent TOAN bombings soon became conflated with fear of any domestic agitation, including hacktivist cyberattacks and peaceful, entirely legal and legitimate street protests in the name of economic justice. This opened wide the door to agents of authoritarian backlash.

And through that door walked the Signals Intelligence Response Service (SIRS), mandated with sweeping powers to monitor and interdict any potential threat to UK national security. With underfunded Scotland Yard in serious decline and private military companies (PMCs) like Albion completely replacing community policing in London, SIRS found itself essentially unchecked on the national security front.

Today, everyone I interview in London assumes their every move is being monitored and logged . . . and, frankly, with few exceptions, this assumption is likely correct. Some approve, some don't. Many fear the intrusion into privacy; others, like the ex-cabbie I met recently in Trafalgar Square, see it as "the only way to track down these filthy foreign animals and terrorists what's swarming London." Remarkable how blind we can be to who the real architects of our misery are, in times of crisis. Civil liberties have taken a seat at the very back of the UK bus, while the driver is domestic security.

CRIME, CRYPTO & THE BLACK MARKET

Another casualty of collapse, of course, is the vaunted British pound sterling. A dominant international currency for centuries, the pound is now in a shocking free fall. As a result, the cryptocurrency E-Token (or ETO for short) has taken London by storm, offering a stable exchange rate against foreign currencies. For many Londoners today, ETO is the only way to stretch their paychecks, since even small fluctuations in the pound can mean being forced to make a beggar's choice among necessities.

While the Bank of England has reluctantly acknowledged ETO, the financial/commercial establishment is fighting to counter its spread, actively stoking fears of cybercrime and attaching an antipatriotic stigma to cryptocurrency transactions. The reason: Using ETO is an untraceable, anonymous transaction, and it can't be stolen from your pocket. Thus, it's even better than cash for making risky black-market purchases.

All of these developments—the widespread job loss, the failure of traditional market forces, the rise of unregulated cryptocurrency— have created the perfect incubator for the birth of a flourishing underground economy. And the raw, unfettered, and illegal nature of black-market trade always plays into the hands of operators guided by purely Darwinian instincts—most especially organized crime.

In London, East End crime culture has been rejuvenated by the collapse of civil society and its marketplaces. Many shady players have jumped headfirst into the rising dark waters, including plenty of formerly legitimate businesses. But surprisingly, it was an old-school family syndicate, Clan Kelley, that quickly consolidated control of the new shadow commerce.

MEDIA, PROPAGANDA & CULTURE

Recently, Britain's beloved GBB television and radio network was privatized and sold off to a foreign media conglomerate. While GBB insists that it remains an impartial reporting outlet, stories have taken on a subtly politicized bent. Features and headlines are groomed to push an agenda that takes a favorable view of SIRS and Albion, while minimizing the severity of London's current problems with organized crime, domestic terror, homelessness, and the crashing pound.

Meanwhile, SIRS has launched SeeSay, a closed social media platform. Users can use the app to report suspicious activity directly to the authorities and are frequently encouraged to do so. All images and other data shared on the platform are monitored (and

occasionally censored) by SIRS agents. As you might imagine, the app has become a favorite cybertarget of hacktivists. So have the 3D holograms, increasingly common in public parks and squares, that deliver "public service messages" encouraging neighbors to snoop and report on one another.

To counter the state's propaganda, Deep Web pirate broadcasts are operating just outside the reach of SIRS and the UK establishment. Irreverent, entertaining, and often quite gonzo, pirate radio has become one of the last outlets where Londoners can hear totally unvarnished opinions and music untainted by corporate interests or SIRS censorship.

CITY LAYOUT

DS-01

ISLINGTON
& HACKNEY
BOROUGH

CAMDEN
BOROUGH

TOWER
HAMLETS
BOROUGH

CITY OF
LONDON

CITY OF
WESTMINSTER

SOUTHWARK
BOROUGH

LAMBETH
BOROUGH

WANDSWORTH
BOROUGH

DS-17

NOTABLE LOCATIONS

NEW SCOTLAND YARD

Even Britain's most stalwart police outpost has been infe
Albion. As the privatized security group has grabbed up i
broad contracts to secure the city, they've managed to ta
much of the investigation and forensic capabilities of Sco
A handful of Met officers, made redundant by Albion staf
established a picket line. Their protest has done a bit to r
visibility and support of just how much Albion has hollow
concept of community policing in London, but from my po
it's too little, too late.

LONDON AUTONOMOUS CARRIAGE SERVI

Perhaps the best proof that nothing is sacred is what's be
of the London black cab service. Black cab drivers were o
renowned for their ability to charm the pants (or, at least,
off tourists with their quick wit and conversationa—as we
possession of "The Knowledge" to navigate the city with
quickness and savvy. That's all gone today. Blume has in
their own knowledge, in the form of a ctOS-powered cent
control AI that monitors vehicles and can pilot any operat
its reach, black cabs included. This high-tech depot serve
primary service and storage garage for the overhauled fle
driverless black cabs in the center of Westminster.

WALKER'S COURT

The gaudy neon of Walker's Court advertises clubs and sho
catering to just about any special interest a wanderer in the
End may hope to indulge. Perhaps the seedy reputation of
has provided a necessary smoke screen, as it's one of a ha
bastions in the area where Albion patrols are less ever-pre
in nearby locations such as Piccadilly Circus or Leicester S
There are even rumours of DedSec congregating somewhe
famous alleyway.

NOTABLE LOCATIONS

CAMDEN MARKET

Tourists rarely brave this once lively market, which has gained a new, dangerous reputation. Clan Kelley has turned the old stables into a tightly guarded black market where the right buyer can find anything from automatic weapons to human organs. Like many of Clan Kelley's criminal hideouts in the city, the market is an open secret that the authorities are either unable or unwilling to address.

BLUME TOWER

Situated in nearby Fitzrovia, Blume's new headquarters in London looms over the city. Their takeover of the Tower was the first highly visible symbol of the chokehold ctOS would eventually gain over all digital communications and infrastructure in London. Far more than a simple telecom antenna, Blume Tower has become equal parts corporate campus and technological compound.

GBB HOUSE

The traditional Marylebone home of England's beloved broadcast network, the GBB headquarters purports to be a bastion of fair and unbiased news reporting and entertainment media production. But this reputation has been tarnished of late. Private interests have gained financial control of the GBB and, according to several leaked communications, asserted editorial influence over every aspect of the organization. Even casual observers have remarked on the shift in GBB coverage, which has begun a dangerous drift toward becoming a mouthpiece for state media.

REGENT'S PARK BARRACKS

With an active land war in Northern Africa and sweeping austerity measures in place, the British Armed Forces are stretched desperately thin. These circumstances have created many opportunities for Albion to grab lucrative contracts and valuable assets as they further integrate themselves into Britain's security apparatus. Their occupation of the Regent's Park Barracks is just one of many ways they've exploited the situation to their advantage. Disturbing rumors have suggested that this location has been especially useful to Albion as a holding facility for illegal detainment within the city.

CARCANI MEDICAL

US pharmaceutical giant Carcani has recently made major investments in the UK wellness industry. Some of that money is invisible to the public, funneled toward lobbyists and politicians. Other investments are very visible, like this automated warehouse for medical supplies and equipment. Pundits point to this as just another sign that private industry is working hard to fully privatize the British healthcare system. Carcani is actively undermining the existing system while carefully positioning itself as a turnkey alternative.

HACKNEY & ISLINGTON

This area is frozen in a moment of transition between the social fringe and modern redevelopment.

NOTABLE LOCATIONS

NEOGATE

The founders of NeoGate saw themselves as the next generation of start-up moguls. Their technology, originally a project at university, would springboard them to the top of the venture capital funding wishlist. The youngsters were fending off acquisition offers from every tech giant in the business and wound up taking an incredibly generous offer from a private firm. If only they'd realized exactly what kind of firm that was. My research into NeoGate has turned up strong links to organized criminals, who seem to be developing their own technology in a secure area of the office that the original founders aren't even allowed access to. I can only imagine what might be going on down there . . .

FINSBURY NEW PROJECT

Let's say, hypothetically, you're trying to run an organized crime firm in London. How do you stay out of the public eye while still operating within the city? Well, if you're part of Clan Kelley, maybe you've realized that construction sites are a perfect candidate for—again, just hypothetically—storing and protecting your stock for a gun-running trade. "What about the workers?" you may wonder? Just find a reason for the project to be stalled (London's all too used to this kind of holdup) and then create as much red tape as possible to ensure work stays halted. The worksite in Finsbury is one such example of a construction project that has seen curiously little construction for months, despite a curiously busy traffic of laden lorries going in and out . . .

STAFFORD AUTO GARAGE

The various legal motions and subsidies that went into the "All of us, Autonomous" campaign were a huge boon for private garage operators like the Stafford family. For months, insurance breaks had encouraged drivers to make their vehicles autonomous-capable with aftermarket sensor installations. But the new legislation made ctOS compliance mandatory. Overnight, garages like this one were suddenly in high demand to install Blume-provided sensor kits in everything from the latest German roadster to rusted-out "classics" that I'm still shocked to see rattling around London with no driver at the wheel. The windfall was short-lived for the Staffords, however, as poor investments of their newfound cash made their garage another victim of Clan Kelley's machinations.

WORLD OF TOMORROW

Just because the city is falling down around their ears doesn't mean that Londoners won't find a way to party. Social hotspots like the World of Tomorrow try to keep the torch burning and provide a shelter in the storm for people who still need a place to eat, meet, and get blind drunk enough to forget the existential nightmare of their everyday lives. Would any of them be surprised, I wonder, to learn that Clan Kelley gangsters are making deals just behind a closed door here? Somehow, I doubt it.

For all of Albion's eagerness to scoop up government contracts to secure swaths of London, the security giant does have its limits. While the business side of the company has scrambled to rapidly staff up and acquire a standing army's worth of hardware, tactical commanders have prioritized their resources to certain parts of the city. This has left places like Tower Hamlets largely unsecured, as Albion patrols and policing are focused elsewhere. While this makes the region a bit of a refuge for those hoping evade Albion's oppressive grasp, the lack of community policing has also left the area wide open for exploitation by the basest sort of criminal.

NOTABLE LOCATIONS

TOWER OF LONDON

Most of us among the living are more likely to remember the Tower as a place we visited on a school trip than as a major military asset. That's all changed today. As Albion's presence in London grew, so did their need for a central headquarters. Their gaze soon fell on what is both the most obvious and most shocking choice: the famous Tower of London itself. Gone are the tourist queues and Royal Beefeaters; for the first time since before the Victorian era the entire site is closed to the public. Behind those walls, Albion has returned the Tower to its darkest days.

BETHNAL GREEN POLICE STATION

The police station at Bethnal Green, like the rest in London today, is staffed with more Albion contractors than actual police. The transition here was slower than most though. The community and workers here protested in defiance when the first Albion employees showed up to work, and Albion was all too happy to respond with a slow financial siege of the station. Requests and requisitions made by Bethnal Green were put at the back of the queue and often ignored entirely. This gradually brought them in line, although the station remains one of the more poorly funded under Albion's management.

ALBION DRONE FACILITY

One of several Albion bases tucked into the unassuming byways of London, this facility is responsible for the maintenance of much of Albion's weaponized drone fleet. The nearby canal was once used to discreetly move drones into the working areas under cover of night; the need for such consideration is long since gone, and Albion is all too happy to work on their drones here at all hours.

WHITECHAPEL TERMINUS

Austerity measures saw the revitalization of this station halted. As the weeks crawled on with no council funding in sight, Whitechapel Terminus slowly become an ad hoc home for the many rough sleepers trying to survive in today's London. Sadly, Clan Kelley saw an opportunity in this, as they have in so much else of the city's suffering. Using the displaced as camouflage, Kelley goons have been seen going in and out of the location, where they have set up shop just steps off the high street, operating their illegal business with impunity.

CITY OF LONDON

The City of London is still home to the financial district of the city, although much of the real fiduciary power has left London entirely, retreating to safer fortresses in Europe and beyond. The hustle and bustle of city life still hums here, albeit with a bit more of an air of desperation than in salad days long gone. Meanwhile, the "ring of steel," which once consisted of subtle hard barriers around the City of London itself, has now proliferated in the form of Albion checkpoints that choke off roadways across all of London in an expensive piece of security theater.

NOTABLE LOCATIONS

CENTRE-UPON-THAMES

While London's fall didn't begin here, many agree that the TOAN attack on the Centre-Upon-Thames exhibition hall is what accelerated matters into today's sad state of affairs. British media was all too happy to ridicule the Technology of All Nations event as the "TOAN-Deaf" conference, and rightly so. Hardly an international showcase, the conference was an obvious and desperate bid by UK technology companies to project an image of intellectual and financial dominance, despite a clear decline in recent years, triggered by austerity measures and widespread brain drain as the UK hemorrhaged skilled engineers, who were attracted to work in other, more stable economies. The ridicule stopped short, however, when the site of the main keynote was destroyed in a shocking attack. The damage done here went far beyond the building itself; the TOAN attack was the final straw upon a fragile sense of security, and Parliament felt pressured to show a swift and decisive response. SIRS and Albion were all too happy to present themselves as the strongmen to answer that call. The rest, regrettably, is not just history; it is our grim present day.

BANK OF ENGLAND

Perhaps the most important qualification to work at the Bank of England today is an ability to stoically ignore the writing on the walls around yourself. Pundits have pointed out that much of the UK's economic woes could have been minimized, had the Bank of England been willing to acknowledge and act upon certain realities more quickly. For example, the Bank of England refused to acknowledge the meteoric rise of E-Token for months. As the pound struggled to stabilize itself in uncertain times, ETO vendors were doing swift business across the city. The wild fluctuations of the pound helped moved cryptocurrency from the fringe to the mainstream; dump your pound into ETO on a good trade day and you were be able to afford groceries while your neighbour struggled to afford crisps just a week later.

BARBICAN CENTRE

Whether you love or hate the distinctive brutalist architecture of the Barbican, it's hard to find much to love about the transformation of the Centre in recent months. A small block of flats here were set aside as temporary housing for potential emigrants awaiting processing. Claiming fear for security on behalf of the Barbican's other residents, Albion set up a surveillance post that has since grown to occupy the once lovely central courtyard. I looked into these claims, of course, and found nothing to back up claims made by an Albion spokesperson that residents have been robbed and harassed since the subsidized flats were set aside. At this point I am beyond feigning surprise.

NOTABLE LOCATIONS

TIDIS

When the American robotics giant opened a UK headquarters at Canada Water, nobody saw the point of it beyond yet another Silicon Valley corporation flexing its muscles with an exorbitant tech campus. The move seemed especially irrational given the fact that many of the engineering grads they'd normally be recruiting were choosing to leave the UK rather than stay and work in London. The connection became much clearer after some documents were leaked, showing the direct connection between Tidis technology and the increased investment in UK surveillance via the drone and robotics technology that Tidis is famous for.

THE NEXUS TOWER

Albion's business development division is the newest resident of one of London's most noticeable skyline landmarks. From their office space in this one highly desirable address, Albion's chief business analysts and strategists chart the roadmap for the company. If they get their way, Albion's martial might will soon be matched by their financial and political influence. It's a chilling idea, but the one thing that gives me comfort is the long list of debtors with whom Nigel Cass got into bed in the early days of the company's growth as he reached well outside his means.

CITY HALL

To say the mayor of London is embattled would be an understatement. The mayor's office has been battered for years by accusations of failure to protect the local communities. The tone and stakes of these complaints have been escalating rapidly. While it seems like unchecked gentrification was the most critical complaint just a few years ago, the wildfire of criminal exploitation, oppressive policing, omnipresent surveillance, and financial instability have created a litany of complaints that see Londoners hurling complaints and insults at the mayor's office daily. Albion has been called in as a standing defense at the perimeter, which has not helped the public's perception of the mayor one bit.

AYW IMPORTS

Clan Kelley's shell businesses are meant to offer the syndicate a superficially legit front to move illicit goods. But the Kelleys are so emboldened lately that they scarcely hide their connections to some of these fronts. Case in point: AYW Imports, an import-export business that ostensibly moves dry goods by waterways between Britain and the Netherlands. Their primary warehouse is just across from the Tate Modern, and tourists have accidentally snapped photos of famous works of art being packed into AYW crates. I'd say these photos cropping up on social media has gone unnoticed, but that's not quite true—the posts have been mysteriously vanishing. Somebody clearly notices, but whether it's a technologically savvy member of Clan Kelley or a powerful ally in the tech industry, I cannot say.

WANDSWORTH

The Nine Elms region was meant to be the real estate developer's dream of London's future: a scintillating strip of redeveloped Thames studded with high-rise offices, embassies, and condominium buildings. The dream came true . . . mostly. Billions of pounds of funding were poured into various construction projects throughout the neighborhood over the past decade or three, and then . . . nothing. As the UK began to stray from the international flock, foreign businesses and investors understandably got cold feet, and many of these projects found themselves suddenly unfunded and abandoned. Some evidence of this is unseen, such as the massive vacancy rates of high-end Wandsworth flats. Certain halted projects, such as the skeletal, half-completed bridge meant to connect Pimlico and Wandsworth, are eyesores and glaring reminders of the impact of the British recession.

NOTABLE LOCATIONS

THE BATTERSEA

What would the coal workers who worked here in the 1950s think of it today? Converted from an industrial landmark to a glitzy shopping gallery, the redesigned Battersea is the very symbol of what developers hoped to craft the Nine Elms into: a shopping center built ostensibly for the public—or at least the "public" with enough disposable income to afford only the highest-end luxury brands and whom pass through the extensive security surveillance to keep undesirables off the property.

SOLAR GARDEN

There's something beautiful about this building, which always makes me smile when I have occasion to pass it in my travels through London. It's one of dozens of ambitious architectural projects that were frozen mid-development by the crashing pound and skittish investors. This one is slowly being reclaimed by nature, as a half-installed arboretum floor has begun to grow wildly out of the incomplete windows and scaffolding. From what I hear, Mother Nature isn't the only one reclaiming the space though—members of a certain crime firm have been spotted coming and going at night. All too common a refrain.

PARCEL FOX DISTRIBUTION CENTRE

What a sweetheart deal the founders of Parcel Fox lucked into—I'm eagerly watching the reporting on who they know, although it seems a hard story to crack. The massive drone facility they've built seems to be punching way above the weight of a tiny start-up that at first seemed much too late to the gig economy party when it was first founded. But somehow Parcel Fox secured one of the only licenses to operate commercial drones in London's airspace when the current drone air control legislation was introduced.

MI-6 BUILDING

SIRS truly catapulted themselves to the top of the British intelligence apparatus after the TOAN bombings. Their sweeping mandate to monitor all signals, domestic and foreign, for signs of impending attack has allowed them to do the unthinkable, usurping powerful agencies that seemed unshakable in their influence. Perhaps the most jarring symbol of this is the prominent occupation of the MI6 building, now emblazoned with a SIRS crest.

9 ELMS DOCKS

Shortly after the TOAN bombing, as part of Albion's desire to create a visible show of force, the Thames was littered with converted barges. These barges, featuring Albion markings and docked combat drones, became an iconic image in the international media in the days following. For Albion, it was the show of force they needed to secure their role as a messianic force for safeguarding London—no matter the cost or the optics. The facility here has become a standing base for Albion's aquatic operations.

The tourist-friendly Thames waterfront transitions into the cultural vibrancy of Brixton.

NOTABLE LOCATIONS

BRIXTON BARRIER BLOCK ESTATE

Like many social programs, the overhauls at this council estate were begun with the best of intentions. As more and more residents found themselves struggling, the grounds of this estate were retrofitted with modular shelters to keep people warm and safe. But those shelters are looking less and less temporary, further eroding already difficult living conditions for the council residents.

ELEK GROUNDS

How remarkable that a famous cricket ground has been converted into a massive housing center for the growing number of Londoners awaiting "processing"—which usually means deportation. The people and families housed here are trapped in a legal limbo that can stretch on for weeks before their status is cleared, during which they're heavily restricted from work and free movement in the UK. Although the government refuses to say the word "refugee," it's hard to think of the people awaiting processing here as anything else.

THAMES PROMENADE

The "Black Jack" flag redesign was strongly rejected across Britain when it was first introduced. Displaying the classic Union Jack became a form of defiance overnight, and the #UnionsFlight protest was the height of this sentiment, as thousands of Black Jacks were stripped from official buildings and replaced by homemade Union Jacks. But strict enforcement laws—and, in this writer's opinion, an outright nationalist propaganda campaign—have all but eliminated displays of the Union Jack, right down to the tacky tourist gear sold in junk shops throughout the city. This is why the merchants at Thames Promenade are considered so bold: The small shopping plaza refuses to let the Black Jack take over, despite repeated fines and arrests. I wonder how long they can keep it up?

E-STROM BUS DEPOT

If Londoners were appalled to see their beloved black cabs replaced by a driverless fleet, wait until they see what E-STROM is working on in their R&D garage. The tech company is quietly toiling away on a replacement for the iconic red bus—just another in a string of lucrative modernization contracts solicited by the government. This project is heavily subsidized by Blume and will include ctOS compliance technology that will funnel even more data about the lives and habits of Londoners directly to the tech giant and their partners.

LEAKE STREET

While this road tunnel under Waterloo might go unnoticed by mainstream tourists, Leake Street is a major stop on any street artist's London pilgrimage. Today, it's one of several impromptu field bases for social programs hoping to house and aid Londoners displaced by the recession or, often, Albion's draconian enforcement protocols.

David:

I typed this on the antique Royal manual that I keep under plexiglass in my office at home. My father wrote his first novel on it . . . which bombed miserably. (He kept the Royal anyway.) He liked this machine because of the factory stamp on the bottom: "Made in Hartford, CT, USA."

But enough personal history. Attached is the agency contact list. These fellows are not happy about what's happening to the services. Focus on KH, BB, and AD. They'll talk off the record, but not on.

Keep it safe. This is your only copy, mate—no electronic version exists.

Cheers,
Louise

PS: I do like how you call me by my surname. I think being just "Hartford" suits me.

AD = Amaichi Davis = MI5 ——> SIRS!!!
Why is he robbing a grocery store?

PART 3

AGENTS OF MASS CONTROL

Good, diligent journalism can be bad for your health. Those old romantic notions of the craft—dark faces lit by cigarettes in underground parking garages, cryptic phone messages, elaborate meeting codes, revelatory "Deep Throat" moments where the back of your neck tingles—well, they actually happen. You run down dead ends, all the time wondering if guys with bone saws and a body bag are waiting for you.

This is London today. Paranoia drifts like fingers of fog. And that's

Most people—by nature, it turns out—want to tell their story, whatever it is. Even secretive people will open the door when properly lubricated with empathy and a few pints of Boddingtons. So, if you wonder how I know some of the more personal takes in this section, just remember two things: I don't reveal sources, and I don't make things up.

SIRS
(SIGNALS INTELLIGENCE RESPONSE SERVICE)
ROLE: COUNTERTERROR AGENCY

SIRS is the UK's new intelligence superagency, tasked with responding directly to any activity deemed hostile as identified by the UK's "signals intelligence" (interception of signals) network. Referred to as "Sirs" by most people who know of its existence (including DedSec and other Resistance groups), the agency refers to itself as "the Service."

Who are they? Many SIRS agents were absorbed from MI5—for better, and for worse. There's a schism inside, as far as I can tell. Agents with a backbone seem to be passed over and pushed to the side in an environment that rewards results at any cost and turns a blind eye to unscrupulous tactics.

My sources show SIRS has developed relationships with London's slimiest far-right, anti-immigrant organization—the English Patriotic Action Front, or EPAF. SIRS appears to be providing them with resources in exchange for intelligence (such that it is). There's even a rumor that a SIRS case officer, operating under the code name "Kingfisher," uses the agency's existing relationship with EPAF leaders to incite targeted violence in immigrant-heavy neighborhoods—an attempt to soften public opinion sufficiently to justify further arrests. It seems that this "Kingfisher" might even be aiming for the bull's-eye: the Kennington Oval deportation camp.

RICHARD MALIK

ASSISTANT DIRECTOR, SIRS

When SIRS was founded, Richard Malik was at the apex of a meteoric rise through the ranks of British intelligence. Despite being only thirty-five, many (including himself) considered Malik the obvious leading candidate for the new counterterror agency's directorship. When the job went instead to an MI5 veteran, Emma Child, he was deeply disappointed. But he took a demotion to work under Director Child, using his experience as a field operative to shape the new agency's operations. Frankly these days Director Child is harder to meet with than the Queen, though her office rewarded me for my persistence by getting me time with Malik. He seemed surprisingly open to talking to a Yank journalist.

DS-17
ii -9000-0 55672108 781

///// 6712-01 *//*9-012   ctOS

KEY TRAITS	Decorous, shrewd, patriotic, ruthless
OBJECTIVES	Provide bold leadership to the British intelligence apparatus
PERSONAL WORLDVIEW	Sees the UK as "Rome, burning"—eroded by moral decay, the interference of foreign interests, and unchecked growth of corporate power

OVERVIEW

Polyglot, computer nerd, and history buff, Malik is fluent in many human and machine languages. He maintains a huge collection of historical (and often obscure) military artifacts: Roman, Ottoman, Byzantine, British, even American. He views global politics as a zero-sum game, and he intends to engineer a British victory.

SIRS
SIGNALS INTELLIGENCE
RESPONSE SERVICE

SPECIAL AGENT

BIO

Richard Malik was raised in South London by his father, a deeply conservative small businessman (a diesel fitter) who died when Richard was a teenager. Malik was an aloof, unpopular teen who excelled in academics on an accelerated track. He spent his spare time absorbing languages: German, French, Spanish, Mandarin, Cantonese, and Arabic, to start. He graduated magna cum laude from college with a degree in political science and rhetoric.

While studying for a masters in computer science, Malik was recruited by the newly restructured Government Communications Headquarters (GCHQ), the security and intelligence organization responsible for providing signals intelligence to the UK's government and armed forces. (This group is most famous for breaking the supposedly unbreakable German Enigma code in World War II.) Malik served as a field officer based in Hong Kong and then Iraq, operating undercover as a software engineer.

During that time, Malik gained a reputation as a skilled and highly disciplined agent, and he was a gifted political operator within the ranks as well. But his field deployment suffered a setback when he was captured and incarcerated in Pakistan for eighteen long, hard months. The ordeal added a grim new level of resolve to his psych profile . . . and a desire to operate more in the darkness, limiting his exposure.

Upon release from a Karachi prison, Malik took no recovery time, instead transitioning immediately to a desk job in a managerial role. Displaying remarkable discipline, he quickly ascended to the post of GCHQ Regional Director of Counterintelligence, Middle East, and he has been quietly rising through the intelligence bureaucracy ever since. After the Newcastle Incident, Malik enthusiastically supported the mission of the new interagency task force with an aggressive cybersecurity stance. The next year, he lobbied hard for Blume Corporation's ISP monopoly, ensuring that all collected data would be fully available to British intelligence.

At the end of our interview, Malik admitted that the recent TOAN bombings had rattled him even worse than his Pakistani imprisonment did. The wanton act crystalized his outrage at the moral decay of England and intensified his sense of urgency.

STRENGTHS

Malik is undeniably brilliant—just ten minutes with him makes that crystal clear—and difficult to fool. Combining wizardly skills in both spycraft and computer security, he has mastered the art of moving in both the physical and organizational shadows. His knack for negotiating bureaucratic structures is due in no small part to the years he spent carefully cultivating an impressive network (both broad and deep) of intelligence contacts.

WEAKNESSES

Malik's manipulations have bred a list of enemies, too. Anyone who opposes him will have natural allies. His hypermoral worldview leaves him prone to dark feelings of disillusionment, which can trigger rare moments of carelessness. Also: With no close family, Malik trusts his inner professional circle far too much for someone in his position.

FEARS

Richard Malik is deeply unsettled by two things: first, the amoral, anarchic, anti-authority worldview of his enemies; and second, any form of direct violence, which he finds messy and unpredictable. (If a death is necessary, he prefers manipulating others into executing the deed.) His greatest fear is failing in his crusade to save the Queen's home realm, since then what will become of his beloved England?

BLUME CORPORATION

ROLE: CORPORATE AI NETWORK

A few years ago, as the British economy slipped off the cliff and began its free fall, the US-based Blume Corporation saw an opportunity to exploit the rising fear and unrest, and it made a strong move into the UK market. To this end, Blume quietly partnered with various high-tech players in the UK, most significantly the brilliant AI software designer, futurist, and entrepreneur Skye Larsen.

The company secured three massive contracts in succession. First, Blume installed its ctOS infrastructure control and surveillance system citywide. Then it deployed its drone-based ctOS network in exchange for a government-authorized ISP monopoly. And finally,

Blume convinced the UK government to mandate universal adoption of its Optik AR system, a personal augmented-reality device that doubles as a metadata collection and telemetric tracking matrix for SIRS.

As a result, Blume is utterly pervasive in London despite operating (as usual) in the shadows and keeping a low corporate profile.

SKYE LARSEN

TECH ENTREPRENEUR/FUTURIST

Inventor of the remarkable (and somewhat frightening) Bagley
AI Companion, a personal digital assistant, Skye Larsen is not
technically a Blume Corporation employee. But she has become
as important to Blume as perhaps anyone in company history.
Her recent start-up, Broca Tech, developed the proprietary
machine-learning algorithms that power the infrastructure and
traffic-control architecture of Blume's ctOS centralized intelligence.

	DS-17
	// 9000 0 55672108 781
	//// 6712-01 //9-012 ctOS

KEY TRAITS	Tech/business genius, affable
OBJECTIVES	Create an AI-driven utopia
PERSONAL WORLDVIEW	Fervently believes that AI is an evolutionary ideal that humankind should strive to achieve

OVERVIEW

Few people know Skye Larsen personally, but one inner-circle
source noted that Larsen's almost cheerful misanthropy gives
her "a twisted Zen-like mentality"—by all accounts, she views
human struggle and suffering with blank detachment. Larsen
cares about money only insofar as it helps fund her visionary
plans. Her notion of an AI-run utopia has fervent opponents, not
all of whom are antitech activists.

Born to Danish-English parents and raised in London's West End, Skye Larsen exhibited a savant-level aptitude for science and math from a very young age. At the same time, she struggled to make friends, showing early symptoms of a misanthropic, verging on sociopathic, nature.

In her final year at university, Larsen formed a start-up company called Broca Tech with some classmates. Larsen herself developed its core product: Bagley, an AI digital assistant considerably more intelligent than other AI interfaces at the time. She sold Bagley to the Blume Corporation for an undisclosed sum (rumored to be in the low nine-figure range), but not before dumbing down its AI into a more subservient and production-ready OS for Blume's Optik protocols.

Larsen continued her refinement of high-level AI and machine-learning technologies with Broca Tech. Her first investment was fairly pedestrian: An automated parking garage system called Matryosh-Car. But subsequent outlays into wildly successful ventures like Tidis and Nudle swiftly expanded her portfolio's worth to almost $1.3 billion, rocketing her to the top of multiple "Top 30 Under 30" lists. Her AI products went on to revolutionize the auton-omous taxi industry (displacing most human drivers) and the admin-istration of the National Health Service (NHS). More ominously, Broca Tech AI forms the neural core of Albion's drone network.

Skye Larsen has become conspicuously absent from the public arena, making infrequent appearances only via hologram technol-ogy. While some see this as typical of her eccentric personality, others believe she may be hiding something. The tabloids? Their headlines proclaim that Larsen is dead, and that Broca Tech is just using the holograms to keep a fire sale on the stock from happen-ing. One such holographic appearance was as keynote speaker at the TOAN conference. Larsen's announcement of plans to engineer a singularity event to usher in an AI-driven perfect world, code-named "Daybreak," was entirely overshadowed by the deadly TOAN bombing.

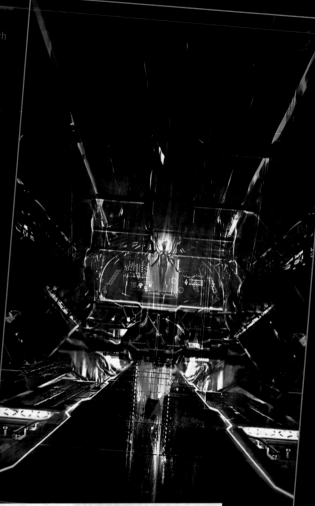

HIGHLY CONFIDENTIAL:

uclh

We are committed to delivering top-quality patient care, excellent education and world class research

Safety
Kindness
Teamwork
Improving

University College Hospital
Autoimmune Disorder Clinic
235 Euston Road
London, NW1 2BU

Patient: Skye Larsen
Attending Physician: Dr. Chandran Banarjee

David—here's where Larsen's lucky streak hits a brick wall. This is not good, mate. Degenerative autoimmune disorder, rare and terminal. Careful with this. I hear her people would kill to keep this secret.

Cheers,

Louise

STRENGTHS

Larsen is a brilliant inventor, programmer, and software developer with a keen business acumen. Her superficial charm, which is considerable, projects an appealing public presence and lets her comfortably navigate relations with difficult people. Her goal-oriented pragmatism lets her make difficult decisions without sentimentality.

WEAKNESSES

Larsen has become a classic hypochondriac and germaphobe, making public appearances only via hologram. Insiders report that she's grown to despise most things associated with human frailty.

FEARS

Very simply: death. My sources suggest that Larsen's utopian dream is driven by raw fear of mortality and the impending decline and extinction of the human species. She uses the twin specters of climate change and overpopulation to sell her futurist AI-driven vision . . . but the truth is, she desperately seeks to set humanity on a track to survive the "great filter" and transcend its current state.

ALBION

Nigel Cass
Power Armor

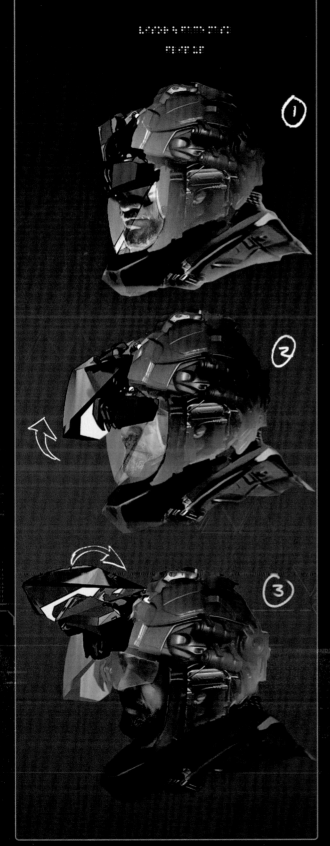

NIGEL CASS

PRIVATE SECURITY CONTRACTOR

Nigel Cass is selling his vast counterinsurgency expertise and his Albion paramilitary regiment to the powerful entities seeking to loot the corpse of London. Incidents like the TOAN bombing play right into his hands: In the Age of Terror, business is booming for private security companies with a track record. Now that London has offered Albion a huge contract to provide consulting and training support for its new military-police initiative, Cass has finally struck the motherlode.

	DS-17

KEY TRAITS	Opportunistic, calculating, cynical, ambitious
OBJECTIVES	Reap the spoils of war and profit from UK's national confusion in the wake of the TOAN bombing
PERSONAL WORLDVIEW	Cass's worldview is purely mercenary and Darwinian—survival of the fittest and most ruthless—with no romantic or family loyalty to England

OVERVIEW

Cass is scion of a celebrated military bloodline, one that reaches back generations into England's glorious martial past. But believing the British Empire to be impotent and dying, he broke the family lineage of distinguished service by jumping whole-heartedly into the murky, mercenary world of paramilitary work for hire. Today, he seeks partners who, like himself, remain unhampered by weaknesses such as morality or respect for tenets of international law.

BIO

Born to Sir Addison and Matilda Cass, Nigel was known on the rugby playing field as physically talented, ruthless, and quick to anger. His flagrant cheating at studies (by paying less-wealthy, more-scholarly students to do his schoolwork) nearly led to his expulsion from prep school and revealed a core character trait: Nigel Cass believes in getting things done without caring *how* they get done.

Upon his graduation, Cass enlisted in the British Army, where he served in the Twenty-Second Special Air Service (SAS) Regiment, an elite Special Forces unit trained in covert reconnaissance, counterterrorism, active resistance, hostage rescue, and other sensitive (and mostly classified) roles. During this time he also honed his skills at procuring contraband items for fellow soldiers and stealing military supplies for sale on the black market.

After his discharge from duty, Cass jumped right into field work for private security firms. A notorious incident in Nigeria turned him into a minor hero: While consulting with energy-industry clients on oilfield and mining security in the Niger Delta, Cass single-handedly foiled a coup attempt by rebel militants associated with the NDLF (Niger Delta Liberation Front).

Upon returning to England, he joined Albion, his father's security firm, as a gold-level executive consultant. When Sir Addison was murdered by one of his own men, Nigel moved fast to consolidate control of the company—over the protests of the Albion board of directors. Under his guidance, Albion quickly became a formidable player in the frenetic landscape of post-Brexit UK power politics.

But lately, old friends and mentors have disavowed Cass and his mercenary dealings . . . a tactical error on their part, given Cass's penchant for settling grudges with brute force.

STRENGTHS

Cass has unshakeable, military-grade confidence, with an iron will to boot. He's also a "true believer"—that is, he truly believes he can bring peace to London, and eventually the world, via brute force and preventative crime measures. Extensive war-zone experience has made him battle-hardened, hunting down foes with relentless patience. He has expert weapons-tech knowledge and a wide network of connections in the black-ops world. Cass wholeheartedly embraces new technologies of war and actively invests money in developing them.

WEAKNESSES

Debt! Albion PMC is a highly leveraged entity. Cass borrowed heavily as he aggressively expanded his investment in state-of-the-art military equipment, and his generous contract offers to topflight ex-SAS personnel have given Albion a clear operational edge in the field. But investor pressure has pushed Cass to seek high-risk, high-reward deals. He's not well suited to civilian life; he's more comfortable in the outback than his posh London flat. His limited understanding of political protocol and his self-imposed lack of a London social network threatens his grand ambitions.

In addition, Cass is brutally distrustful. Nigel Cass revered his father, Sir Addison, the original founder of Albion. A compassionate man, Sir Addison was fond of rehabilitating criminals, giving them a new sense of purpose within Albion's ranks. That is until one of those same criminals betrayed the old man, assassinating him right in front of his son. Nigel's faith in the goodness of humanity appears to have died along with his father.

FEARS

CLAN KELLEY

ROLE: ORGANIZED CRIME FIRM

London's organized crime clans—known as "firms"—are typically family-run operations rising up in tough, impoverished working-class neighborhoods. Clan Kelley, a storied East End firm with roots in Northern Ireland, took advantage of the post-Brexit chaos to move aggressively into cryptocurrency markets and leverage that into control of the city's rapidly growing underground economy—from old standbys like prostitution, drugs, and weapons into the staples of life: commodities like food and water, furniture and electronics, and anything else you'd buy on Amazon or Craigslist. But Clan Kelley's biggest (and most insidious) "services" innovation has come in the area of human trafficking.

MARY KELLEY

CRIME BOSS

Mary Kelley, daughter of Clan Kelley's legendary founder, Peter Kelley, has become the most powerful and feared crime boss in London since the days of the notorious Kray brothers. In many ways she has surpassed those predecessors. Under her brilliant leadership, the Kelley family firm has transformed almost overnight into a modernized cybercrime syndicate, operating at scale, with unmatched reach into sectors of the economy beyond the usual purview of organized crime.

DS-17

ctOS

KEY TRAITS	Motherly, attentive, cutting, ruthless
OBJECTIVES	Restore Clan Kelley to former glory through ironclad control of the black market
PERSONAL WORLDVIEW	Tough life favors the aggressor, always, and right now, the UK crime scene is ripe for the taking

OVERVIEW

Oversaturated with old men struggling to maintain old power relationships and old transactional systems, London's under-world is quickly succumbing to Mary Kelley's overhaul efforts. The emigration crisis and collapsing economy under the new oppressive regime has provided the opening she needs, as millions now rely on London's black market for essential goods, not just illicit services.

Mary is the daughter of Peter Kelley, legendary East End crime boss, and she grew up steeped in the family business. Peter, bitterly disappointed that his wife never bore him a son, always tried to keep Mary on the outside due to her gender. When Mary turned eighteen, Peter suggested she "play her part in growing the firm" by marrying into another East End crime family, the Mohan Clan. She dutifully wed Patrick Mohan, an abusive drunk. Mohan ended up dead a few months later—many suspected Mary, but no one openly accused her. Still, before the man died, he left Mary pregnant with a son, Johnny.

The boy turned out rather dull and dim-witted, but his grandfather doted on him, grooming Johnny to take his place as head of Clan Kelley. Meanwhile, Peter put Mary in charge of the family's books due to her talent with numbers. As a result, she gained a deep understanding of the syndicate's financing and infrastructure.

When Peter was given a fifty-year prison sentence for drug trafficking, Mary seized the opportunity to take control of the organization. She swiftly modernized the business, bringing it into the digital age. Within a year, Clan Kelley established a commanding presence in the dark-web black markets, and Mary led aggressive moves to consolidate all East End criminal activity under the Kelley umbrella. After Brexit's turmoil tanked the pound and drove most citizens to cryptocurrencies for greater security, Mary engineered ingenious ways to lure those funds into dark-web transactions.

STRENGTHS

Mary Kelley can exude genuine Irish warmth, and her motherly manner can be disarming. She notices everything—that you shaved or got a new tie, what your favorite footballer or soda is, and if you have a cocaine problem or a thing for redheads. No detail escapes her gaze. Those details come in handy when she wants something from you. Also: Mary's not afraid to get her hands wet. Her nickname—Bloody Mary—comes from her penchant for dispatching enemies at close quarters with a knife, an activity

WEAKNESSES

Mary always does what she believes is best for the firm, even if it means pain for those in her immediate circle, including family. Thus, despite her people skills, she can overlook the obvious human element in certain situations, especially if it's one she wasn't expecting. Foes who know this can capitalize. She rules through fear, and thus few in Clan Kelley's rank and file feel a genuine sense of loyalty to her. Mary is particularly despised by her army of indentured servants, most of whom she treats with

FEARS

Mary Kelley is a control freak—certainly understandable, given her life. Her rough, brutish upbringing has expunged most basic human fears from her outlook. She isn't afraid of violence, hate, betrayal, or isolation. But she gets rattled when she feels herself losing her grip—such as when something happens that she didn't plan or can't directly control.

PART 4

RESISTANCE RISING

Beyond the major players in London, many more forces are still in hiding, waiting to be uncovered. The antiauthoritarian movement in London is beginning to take shape. Its emergence has been swift and truly remarkable—a thoroughly modern insurgency.

You see it everywhere, even in neighborhoods considered Albion strongholds. Witty street art lampooning the police state pops up overnight in very public, highly surveilled places. Spontaneous protests and brilliant street-theater "demonstrations" ebb and flow across the city. Albion has no more chance of stomping them all out than it does flushing the duckweed from Limehouse Basin.

Again, cheeky British defiance in the face of threat and oppression is one of those things you can always count on. It's a verity of history. Britain will never go quietly into the dark night of tyranny.

But not since the English Civil War of the 1600s has there been such a sharply polarized split in the nation's politics. Tendrils of fear and outrage have entangled every district of London.

Signals Intelligence Response Service
Field Assignment: 03927667
Operative: Amaichi Davis, FO9229

Criminal Activity Reported:	Location:
Organized, small-scale food smuggling operation	South Bank, London

Victim:
Local grocer/restaurant network

Suspects:
Gang elements (Gabriel's Wharf)

Witness/Intel Sources:
* SeeSay input tickets
* SBS Citizen Patrol reports
* Corroboration: CCTV (SB40 archive)

A. Davis originally transitioned to SIRS from
MI5 as Senior Intel/Ops Director, Unit 4

Now he's a field grunt? SERIOUS DEMOTION!

EXCLUSIVE

FUTURE SOUNDS OF LOND

Smart City Grid Grabs Wrong Car
AI Glitch Kills Two Civilians in Police Chas

Two unsuspecting London motorists careened to fiery deaths in the West End Tuesday when the city's automated traffic system mistakenly commandeered their retrofitted compact car and sent it hurtling into Marble Arch during a harrowing, high-speed police chase.

The deceased were identified as Tad Bevins and Mo Saladin, two bloggers working for the Daily Monstrosity, an unsanctioned online site known for dark-web activity. The pair was traveling to a dinner meeting with friends when centralized Smart City computers seized control of their vehicle for a wild pursuit in progress.

"The city recently deployed a new fleet of compact cars designed specifically for urban pursuit scenarios," said Harold Hunter, SIRS service liaison with London's integrated law enforcement authority. "The vehicle in question appears to have been mistakenly entered into the ctOS database."

The chase, initiated by an Albion security team, had targeted suspected IRA terrorists traveling toward a location that Scotland Yard refuses to disclose. (It remains classified as of this writing.) Scans of citizen-generated Optik videos recorded along the route suggest chase speeds in excess of 90 kph along some of London's major thoroughfares.

D: These "bloggers" were first-rate investigative reporters with contacts inside SIRS. They had disgruntled former MI5 agents—bad culture, rogue ops in the service. Tad and Mo were also my friends.

This was no glitch, mate. This was SIRS and Albion sending a message. Watch your back.

— Louise

UNDER THE DEDSEC UMBRELLA

In the early days, DedSec was one of numerous ad hoc groups banding loosely together to form London's collective Resistance. But then the original DedSec London "chapter" mysteriously disappeared after the TOAN bombing. This led to a remarkable development.

Rumors of what happened to DedSec went viral. The name DedSec soon took on an almost mythic quality. At the same time, other DedSec chapters in New York, Amsterdam, Berlin, and elsewhere began to focus on the disappearance. Eventually, a new wave of activities took up the DedSec moniker, using it as a rallying cry against the fascists and disaster profiteers corrupting London.

INSIDE THE MOVEMENT

Over the past twelve months I've met and interviewed dozens of DedSec operatives, studied their direct-action tactics, and reviewed their internal collection of vlogs and written manifestos.

At first, I was somewhat surprised to discover that almost nobody I met seemed concerned that I might reveal important secrets. Over time, I learned why . . . and I feel confident in stating that nothing in this book will compromise DedSec operations.

The first reason: DedSec ops planning is so random and decentralized (and downright *vaporous*) that it would be nearly impossible to betray its structure or methods to authorities. SIRS might as well try to scatter-plot the Perseid cloud to predict the exact particle spread of the next meteor shower.

The second reason: DedSec's unrivaled expertise at hacking and scrubbing London's ctOS-based surveillance grid—the cameras and tracking drones, the recognition software—means its operatives typically leave no trail to follow. My SIRS contacts have confirmed this. Something crazy happens in the real world . . . but then the signal data says no, it didn't.

ORGANIZATION & TACTICS

While not entirely leaderless, DedSec bears resemblance to radically democratic groups like Occupy Wall Street—individual members are empowered to take initiative and then encouraged to act. Plans evolve, ad hoc, in an instant. In the meantime, DedSec members continue to live their lives, blending in with the population of the city, keeping their eyes open and staying ready to act when the time is right.

Teams gather, protest, and dissipate with flash-mob speed. Pirate podcasts spread via zombie botnets, suddenly disappear, then reappear on the dark web. SIRS and even Blume can only react from four steps behind.

Typically, DedSec activists operate independently or form small cells that loosely coordinate in shifting, organic alliances. Chaotic as that "distributed model" can be, it is highly effective, particularly in dense urban settings . . . as proven time and again by both ancient and modern history.

The original DedSec had a nonviolent ethos. Today, many DedSec black bloc cells employ "active resistance techniques"—that is, they shoot back, albeit typically with "less-than-lethal" (LTL) weaponry. However, few observers other than SIRS would brand them terrorists, or even ideologues. The clear motivation is to counteract the egregious injustice and thuggish suppression tactics perpetrated by the modern authoritarian surveillance state in London.

Of course, this puts a big bull's-eye target on DedSec's back. Local authorities now consider the group a major threat; known operatives and affiliated cells are labeled as wanted criminals.

PROFILES: DEDSEC OPERATIVES

The newly emerging DedSec collective in London is a crazy crosshatch of wildly different personalities and motives that, more and more, intersect in an activist headspace calling itself "DedSec." In seeking to construct a comprehensive dossier on the group, I spent months exploring the boroughs of London, tracking down tips and rumors (some solid, some not so much), leaving a trail of contact cards and, most importantly, trying to build trust.

Eventually, my history of fair reportage and my network of longtime DedSec contacts in America helped me get a foot inside the blast door of the DedSec London core cell. There, I gained access to a wide variety of folks in the field. Calling them "agents" or "field operatives" might have some generic validity, but the movement is far more freelance than such labels would suggest.

NOTE: All names listed are pseudonyms, and while based on actual photo images, none of the portrait sketches are photorealistic depictions. Key identifying features have been altered to thwart Blume recognition software.

NOTE: All DedSec operative profiles show only one image since we are interviewing one person.

"ANARCHO-SOCIALIST"

NAME: Maya   **AGE:** 24

Articulate and passionate, Maya's a natural leader. She embodies millennial disenfranchisement and holds radical views on how to attack London's current problems. When I stepped into her East End flat, she greeted me by saying, "Incremental change is bullshit." It's all or nothing for Maya, and if that means tying on a bandanna and punching some fascists, so be it.

Boisterous, erudite, irreverent, defiant, dismissive, darkly funny, and brutally honest (even offensive), Maya has no time to coddle egos. Example: During our interview, she received a phone call from a younger compatriot. After a few curt yes/no responses, she sighed and said, "It's not my job to bring you up to speed on these things, mate. Read a fucking book. I've got a few you can borrow."

Despite Maya's deep knowledge of politics and society, her manner is pure street. Maybe it's a bit of affectation, or maybe it's because "professional demeanor" is just a tool of the oppressive classes. Whatever the case, Maya is DedSec because she wants to fight, literally.

One of Brendan's fellow DedSec cell mate
told me: "He acts like an ignorant lout. He
is not." It didn't take me long to pick up on
that. Surprisingly articulate with a cutting
wit, Brendan is anything but stupid. One
clue: The sad-eyed bouncer keeps a
dog-eared copy of Voltaire's *Candide* in a
pocket of his gym bag. In fact, he reads
widely, keeps abreast of current events,
and has an unerring bullshit detector.

Over ales served at cellar temperature,
Brendan explained to me how a tumul-
tuous Cornwall home life and dyslexia
set him up for failure in school. Scrawny
before an early-adult growth spurt, he
was bullied relentlessly until he ran away
to London, where he survived by taking a
job at a Marylebone boxing gym run by the
Irish mob. There, he learned to take care
of himself . . . and when he grew and thick-
ened, any semblance of bullying stopped.

This deep hatred of bullies and thugs
like Albion led him soon enough to Ded-
Sec. Outwardly stoic and cool, Brendan
has an angry fire burning inside. Combine
that with his aggressive sense of loyalty
to his running mates, and as one attested,
"He will eviscerate anyone who tries to
fuck with him or his." His cell always
looks to him when they need straight-up
advice . . . or some skulls cracked.

"PRAGMATIC PUNK"

| NAME: Shawna | AGE: 19 |

Raised in a council estate, Britain's version of a public housing complex, Shawna was a smoker at twelve, dropped out of school at fourteen, and at fifteen received her first IPNA—or an "injunction to prevent nuisance or annoyance" (a civil power in Britain designed to deal with antisocial behavior). Coarse, loud, and so over it, she's been around the block more than once.

When she turned sixteen, Shawna took a court-ordered job, working the counter at a McDonald's in North London. She says she even liked it, for a while. But the twenties' wave of automation made her redundant, like so many others. On her last day she robbed the restaurant blind and vanished into London's street life.

That's when she learned, as she explained simply, "Freedom is happiness." She survives by dabbling in everything from app gigs to clever grifts—anything to keep from getting tied down. Alternately brash and charming, she has learned how to work the streets with brutal finesse.

But with cameras and jackboots on every corner now, it's getting harder and harder to stay independent and out of jail. So Shawna joined DedSec to take advantage of the extra breathing room that gives her—and maybe bring a little breathing room to the world.

AGE: 4

Bogdan may
animated by
him apart fr
a naïve drea
times. Raise
authoritaria
Europe (he
explains tha
Western act
to everyday
shooting, an

"It seemed
each a shot
Gold. "Why
guys?" Afte
put him at o
his motherla
emigrated w

At first, says
by the xenop
seemed to f
and he fell i
eyes open, a
to become t
always want
And while h
cinematic in
at the punch

"HEDONIST"

NAME: Oscar   **AGE:** 41

A libertine with a vicious smirk, Oscar simply has no time in his schedule for shame or moderation. He's too busy adding to his collection of vices: "sweeties" (recreational drugs), fine liquors, sex, and sport cars. And as he explained to me over drams of Louis XIII in a posh Chelsea bistro, "DedSec is the best new drug there is." (He also told me: "Chap, what's the point of being wealthy if you can't wallow in corrupt luxuries?")

Oscar openly admits that he'll hit on anything with a pulse, and he's always ready to unsheathe a razor-sharp barb. But his dandy persona doesn't stop him from getting his hands dirty if necessary. He's is proud to point out that he's ruined Brioni suits in sacrifice to the DedSec cause. And you don't want to meet the sharp end of his custom-modified Burberry umbrella.

But after a couple of conversations, I got the distinct sense that Oscar's addictive personality is also numbing something: the feeling that maybe he doesn't really deserve all this money and privilege. DedSec ops may be the best drug he's ever tried, but they're also a chance for him to earn a more or less honest place at the table. Not that he'd ever admit it.

"SEER OF THE APOCALYPSE

AGE: 21 | **NAME:** Hoffman

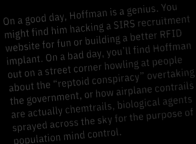

On a good day, Hoffman is a genius. You might find him hacking a SIRS recruitment website for fun or building a better RFID implant. On a bad day, you'll find Hoffman out on a street corner howling at people about the "reptoid conspiracy" overtaking the government, or how airplane contrails are actually chemtrails, biological agents sprayed across the sky for the purpose of population mind control.

I have to say, my meeting with Hoffman was one of the more fascinating interviews I've conducted. Yes, he's the stereotype of an oddball paranoid genius. Like many geniuses, he cares about the world as an abstract concept. But talking to him, I was struck by something else. Sure, he gets upset and rants when his own people dismiss his crazier ideas. But that's because Hoffman genuinely cares about his own people. He truly wants to save his friends from the reptilian overlords.

Even if Hoffman's villains are science-fictional and his fears are paranoid, Hoffman's compassion is real-world. And as it turns out, Hoffman's dedication to disruption of the authoritarian state is one of DedSec's best weapons, an ace in the hole.

BAD NEWS, MATE. MY SOURCES TELL ME THEY NABBED YOUR FRIEND, THAT NAILS-HARD LADY, MS. HARTFORD. I LIKE HER. SHE DOES GOOD WORK. HER "DISPATCHES" ARE SMART. YOU NEED TO MOVE FAST IF YOU WANT TO SAVE HER BRAIN MATTER. REPTOIDS DON'T WAIT LONG BEFORE THEY FEAST.

CHEERS,

HOFFMAN

"TIGHT-ASS BASTARD"

NAME: Ian	AGE: 31

A former officer in the UK army, Ian is a natural leader, but he sometimes clashes with the rest of his cell over his rigid discipline and old-school methods. Our meeting in a Chelsea pub was somewhat tense—he's by nature wary, cold, fatalistic, and somewhat misanthropic. But when I heard his story, it all made sense.

In Afghanistan, Ian witnessed several soldiers in his unit dismembered by a massive IED (improvised explosive device). He can't share details for fear of outing his identity, but he now struggles with symptomatic PTSD almost daily. The incident and the military's response to it left him deeply disillusioned. Finding DedSec, he says, saved his life.

"I do, however, despise this organization's sloppy, ad hoc methods," he admitted.

But knowing Ian's story gives his Ded-Sec crew perspective on his obsessive attention to detail and tight coordination on every operation. I was struck by their good humor and tolerance of his somewhat terse, unpleasant manner when discussing tactical issues with his team. "He's tough, but not unreasonable," said one. "None of us wants to end up in a SIRS black site."

When Sarah enters a room, the first thing she does is subtly locate all the exits. A former Spetsnaz officer (the name for special purpose military and police units in Eastern Europe), Sarah became a private security contractor and had a long and varied career protecting politicians, celebrities, and high-profile executives. Many of her clients were not good people. Some, in fact, were very bad people. This drove her from the business and left her awash in guilt.

Over Earl Grey tea and Scottish shortbread, Sarah told me that fighting with DedSec now gives her a moral clarity she been seeking her whole life. Naturally, her Spetsnaz training makes her a highly skilled fighter. She knows how to blend into a crowd and read complex situations quickly. And her background opens a window of insight into Albion tactics and training—valuable intel for DedSec in general and for Sarah's cell of comrades in particular.

Efficient, calculating, always on the lookout, while observing and assessing everything, Sarah has a naturally protective nature. Her sober professionalism sometimes clashes with DedSec's more anarchist elements—but no matter how much her local crew gets on her nerves, she'll defend them with her life.

Catherine's story is legendary among the locals. For twenty years, this beloved, friendly, vulgar, but supremely clever woman was queen of DedSec's favorite backwater hangout—we'll call it the Harp & Heron. Catherine became a community touchstone as owner, bartender, in-house shrink, and (sometimes) bouncer. Folks haunted the Harp as much for her gossipy monologues as her taste in ales and lagers.

I met Catherine on a park bench in Mount Street Gardens, and we shared slugs of Crown Royal from her pewter flask. ("I like a good Canadian," she told me slyly.) She recounted how she inherited the pub when her father died, dragging the place out of debt by working out a deal with local gangs. Instead of paying protection money, the Harp kept a special safe under the floorboards for what she called "local proceeds." Catherine became, in effect, the neighborhood bank and laundry—with a reputation for being honest, fair, and very discrete.

Nobody expected her to be such a tough, daring businesswoman. But the Harp became a popular place of solace mainly due to her personal warmth. Unfortunately, two years ago, SIRS busted the local criminal organization and seized her pub. Now it's a health food joint, something she considers an abomination.

After a year of forced retirement spent watching the creep of corruption across the district, Catherine began to look for a way to fight back. Her former DedSec clientele realized that her interpersonal skills and extensive network of trusted local contacts would prove invaluable. Today, she said, "It's a match made in heaven, love."

AGE: 35 | **NAME:** Niki

Brave, bold, boisterous, and up for anything with a measurable thrill factor, Niki doesn't have much time for political dithering. When I asked about her personal goals, she said she just wants to jump a Maserati over the Thames. When I asked why, she stared at me, confused, then said: "Why not?"

Niki grew up in Mumbai and admits she spent her twenties wandering the world, looking for "great capers and great parties." Initially, she was lukewarm about London and nearly left after a year. But things got interesting in the Brexit aftermath. In fact, the worse things got on the street, the better Niki liked it. She started finding good "delivery" gigs as the black market heated up, and her fearless driving skills drew attention.

"I fell in with DedSec by accident," she said. "Literally."

During a street race, Niki power-drifted around a tight turn and rebounded off the front fender of a DedSec operations van on Piccadilly. Now she runs some of the crew's craziest ops. If you're hitting an Albion armored patrol and need a surefire getaway, better call Niki.

Yes, Raymond—one of my favorite interviews—is tired. Hard-edged, strict, and impatient, Raymond finds many (okay: most) of his younger counterparts annoying. They're either bleeding-heart pansies or bumbling hard-ass wannabes.

"All I wanted was some peace and quiet, but the country just had to go and screw itself again," he said. "And now, the only people interested in doing something about it are these packs of young DedSec idiots who seem just as likely to blow it all up." After a long swallow of his black and tan, he continued. "I'm too old for this shit, but someone's got to keep an eye on them."

Raymond isn't really interested in playing father figure to anyone, but he finds he sometimes has to wade in and "smack some sense into these morons." His attitude is: DedSec needs to learn that everything in life is a fight, so shut up, get tough, and let the old-timer show you how it's done.

AGE: 32 | **NAME:** Clementine

Smooth-talking and cool even with a gun in her face, Clementine knows that a little charm is often the best weapon in your go bag. Walking down a service alley near her DedSec crew's South Side turf, she sounded like a university professor: "Calculated verbal engagement can facilitate a clean solution to a problem." Clementine says she always prefers discretion to gunplay.

But sometimes, calculated verbal engagement is also the best way to get a clean shot—or as she put it, "cull the weak." Despite her calm demeanor, Clementine is a straight-up badass with a sniper rifle. Her mastery of military-grade gear and high-velocity ballistics provides a huge benefit to her operations team.

She comes off a bit jaded in an interview, but her team says it's a well-practiced demeanor. "If someone knows how much you care about something, it gives them leverage," explained one of her housemates.

"DETERMINISTIC"

My DedSec contact had some words of warning as we stood at the safe-house door. "Bronwen is a genius, and I don't use that word lightly," he said. "She's also an insufferable asshole." When I asked how so, he explained: "She'll be impatient with the speed of your central processor." He pointed at my head.

Boy, was he right. The woman has no time or inclination to be polite or share her knowledge with stupid people—that is, anybody else. But, as I eventually learned, Bronwen cannot help being this way. She's a high level 2 on the autism spectrum. For her, social norms are perplexing. So she's accepted who she is: blunt and socially inept, unintentionally funny sometimes, and brilliant.

Truth be told—and Bronwen always tells the truth—she joined DedSec only because, in facing such long odds against such powerful institutional foes, the group has the most interesting problems to solve. But she does not take a nuanced approach to problem-solving. As a result, she has a way of enraging people. Some compatriots wonder if her deep understanding of Blume's machine learning and its limitations is worth the aggravation. The answer: Yes, it is.

AGE: 33 | **NAME: Lucy**

Born and bred in Chelsea, Lucy is young, cruel, cold, ruthless, vindictive, adversarial . . . and extremely wealthy. Heir to a privately held equity holdings fortune, she's never had to work a day in her life. Yet she runs her own small design studio, anyway—apparently, according to some sources, just for the fun of abusing subordinates.

Our interview was like a root canal for both of us. Perpetually unimpressed with others, Lucy speaks in sharp, dry, staccato syllables. I noted that she particularly enjoys slipping long, awkward pauses into conversation. Clearly, she likes watching people squirm.

Given her psychology, you might wonder why Lucy has deigned to join DedSec, or why DedSec would let such a sociopath anywhere near one of their operations. Two big reasons: money and access. Lucy deeply despises the Albion goon squads she encounters in Knightsbridge every day and her financial infusions provide critical support for DedSec operations against the philistine squads.

And Lucy's family connections can get her in the door almost anywhere that filthy-rich power brokers gather. Her role as an inside operative has been invaluable for DedSec intelligence ops.

"DYING REALIST"

NAME: Beatrix | **AGE:** 73

Wise, pithy, and compassionate, Beatrix is a cunning matriarch who has learned to affect a "sweet old Gran" persona to hide her razor-sharp mind and calculating agenda. She hurries for no one, suffers no fools, and struggles to be patient with her younger counterparts, often breaking character to curse a ghastly blue streak when frustrated.

"Good god, I'm old enough to remember Cold War Europe," she said. "We sat on the precipice of authoritarian control and barely escaped by the skin of our crooked yellow teeth." Then she pointed at me. "Are you going to save us? I can't count on you to properly wipe yourself, much less save your own arse."

Thus, Bea sees this fight as her duty to her country, her Queen, and especially her grandchildren. She's determined to make a difference while she still can. If that means slipping something nasty into the Albion tea, then so be it.

"WENDELL"

AGE: 31 | **NAME:** Responsible

A patient man of Caribbean ancestry, Wendell would greet his worst enemy with a warm smile and firm handshake. Years spent organizing in the trade union movement have made him an expert peacemaker—and even better at concealing his true feelings. He approaches DedSec ops with the same rigorous professionalism he applies to his work.

Thoughtful and easy to talk to, Wendell often finds himself falling into leadership roles, even if he'd rather call himself something less hierarchical, like a "facilitator" or an "administrator." But the fact is, people like and trust him easily, and he's learned not to take that responsibility lightly.

"IRREVERENT OPTIMIST"

NAME: Kris	AGE: 18

Kris has dealt with enough authority figures in his short life to know they're all full of crap. Most of them don't even believe in the corrupt, self-serving system they're perpetuating. He laughs in the face of anyone stupid enough to tell him what to do.

After dropping out of school at age twelve, Kris picked up an unorthodox street-level education. His ideas tend to be unconventional at best and impossible at worst. However, his raw energy level makes up for a lot of miscalculation.

He's quite bright (but not obviously so) and offers up amusing observations and theories, which appear daft at first but improve upon further consideration. He's also the life of the party, intent on teaching DedSec how to enjoy themselves while staging their glorious insurgency.

AGE: 36 | **NAME:** Connor

Connor is a connoisseur, and his watch-word is style. Affable and a bit silly, he's a charming joker who loves being the center of attention. He always knows exactly how to command a room—heavy on the slang, lots of knowing humor. His disarming, jovial manner puts people at ease, and his natural charisma puts him into leader-ship roles.

"Everything Connor does, everything he says, it's all cool, man," said his girl-friend, Mackenzie, part of his DedSec cell. She laughed, adding, "He's always ready for a crep check." More importantly for the crew . . . whatever you ask of Connor, no matter how tough or dangerous, he's down. His joker persona is a clear gloss over fearless grit.

"WOKE AUTOMATON"

NAME: Jess   **AGE:** 23

Hardworking, competent, type-A Jess is a model citizen who once believed that if you worked hard and did your best, you would be rewarded. Top student in computer science, hired right out of school by a Nine Elms tech giant, Jess worked her way up the company ladder to the position of technical support manager—all in accordance with her five-year plan.

But then her mother got sick, and smart Jess learned something new. "One setback can tear your life completely apart," she told me. "And nobody cares."

Now Jess passionately believes that the people of London are being exploited, marginalized, automated into redundancy, and placed in no-win situations so greedy corporations can profit. It's a simplistic belief, but powerful, and certainly not untrue.

Burning with a desire to protect her family and other people like her, Jess is now applying her considerable smarts and persistence to the DedSec mission, so Londoners get a fair shot at a better quality of life.

"NEEDS A SMOKE"

AGE: 52	NAME: Arthur

Grizzled, fatalistic Arthur is that chewed-up, working-class chain-smoker you often meet in the corner pub, the guy who tells you his life story for a fresh pint. You've probably heard his story before, but it's so full of tragic detail that it sucks you in.

Arthur almost played for a big football club out of school, but he couldn't quite make the cut. Then he was a dad, but now his kids are grown and gone. He once owned a pub like the one where we met, but a Nando's restaurant bought and gutted it. And that's where the story gets interesting.

The bad state of London hits blokes like Arthur hard, and he decided to do something about it. He joined up with the high-tech Resistance group DedSec. But if you want to know about the stuff they have him doing . . . well, that'll cost you another round.

TRANSCRIPT OF FOLLOW-UP INTERVIEW WITH "ARTHUR":

At his request, I met Arthur again two months after our first chat—I can't reveal where. He was clearly wary and at times hesitant to reveal information. Here's the key exchange:

INTERVIEWER: So your informants are police officers?

ARTHUR: Formerly.

I: *What are they now?*

A: Albion goons. *[laughs]* Work is hard to come by, mate, what with all the robots.

I: *But you trust them?*

A: Yes, sir. Bar mates. Good men. *[pauses]* We have quite the history, some of it very shameful. *[laughs]* *[To the barkeep:]* Two more pints, ——.

I: *How do they feel about Albion taking over all the community policing?*

A: *[flash of anger]* It's bollocks, is what it is.

I: *Is that how they feel or how you feel?*

A: It's how *everybody* feels.

I: *What is this "item of interest" you mentioned in your message?*

A: Right, that little grocery incident in South Bank last week. You know, where drones turned a robber into hamburger meat.

I: *The Amaichi Davis killing.*

A: Yes. Did Ms. Hartford tell you about him?

I: *Wait. You know Louise Hartford?*

A: *[annoyed]* We all do.

I: *Do you know where she is?*

A: No, but we're looking, mate, we're looking.

I: *Louise guided me to information revealing Mr. Davis to be a SIRS field agent.*

A: Former MI5.

I: *Right. And he was not happy about SIRS policy and procedure.*

A: My boys were in a backup team for them Albion blokes who took him out. They went there looking for Davis. They *knew* he was in there.

I: *[pause] Albion knew Amaichi Davis was at Highpoint Foods?*

A: Yes.

I: *How?*

A: Little phone call from SIRS. Davis gone rogue, they says, a danger to Her Majesty and the realm.

I: *[pause] Can I buy you another pint?*

BRAVE
NEW TECH

Technology has always played a crucial role in the modern power struggle between the forces of authoritarianism and of resistance. From the police state's armored columns and riot gear to the street

Today, London has become the testing ground of a new generation of mass surveillance and population control technologies. Such technologies of control tend to operate in the realm of fear. Psy-

EVERYDAY TECH

Optic Resonance Display: Blume's breakthrough is a technology called "afferent-cutaneous resonant interfacing," which allows Blume to develop an implant capable of sending complex signals directly to the nervous system without the need for invasive surgery. The first efforts focused on communication with the optic nerve, allowing Blume to render digital images directly to the human brain. The system also uses the inner ear as a sort of native accelerometer, allowing the device to track head movements, crucial for Blume's interface solutions.

Blume billed its semipermanent dermal implant as no more invasive or risky than a simple ear piercing. To the surprise of market analysts everywhere, the device became widely popular.

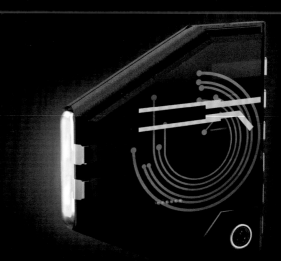

"Privacy, Assured": One of the big selling points of Optik's integrated AR is privacy and exceptional security. This is not really true, of course: The Optik system relies on rapid packet exchange between its base unit (which handles cell/data transmission and general processing) and the optic display implant (which is mostly a dumb relay), and heavy encryption on that traffic is prohibitively complex.

To achieve acceptable latency, this data is unencrypted, making Optik AR highly susceptible to packet sniffing. (This is what DedSec hacking software does on ping, exposing the Optik AR displays of others nearby.) These vulnerabilities have been greatly downplayed by Blume, despite being identified by security experts.

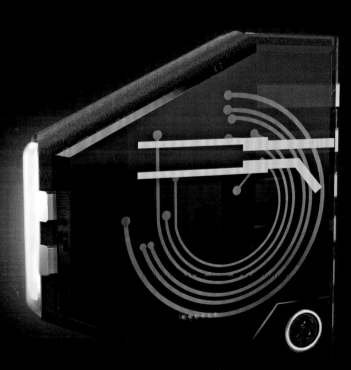

OPTIK 2.0

MANUFACTURER: BLUME

OPERATORS: ALL CITIZENS

SPECS

3mm post implant, inserted to front part of ear

Optik main processor, attached over skin via neodymium magnet

SPECS

SeeSay is a Blume app that encourages users to document suspicious activity and report it directly to SIRS. DedSec has called it an "Orwellian Instagram"—when users sign up, they get a catchy spy handle and avatar. Users whose reports generate actionable intelligence get badges to display on their profiles. All such reports are displayed in a public dossier to be "commended" (i.e., liked) and discussed by other users. Insidiously, there is no penalty whatsoever for filing a false report.

The UK's Home Office runs SeeSay's pervasive ad campaign, with the broad objective of supporting SIRS by crowd-sourcing surveillance data. Another objective: Londoners see constant reminders that they're being watched, even by one another. These reminders come in the form of posters, advertisements, and public announcements; news, talk, and crime fiction shows; and cross promotion with other apps.

BE VIGILANT.
ALWAYS.

SECURELONDON

IF YOU SEE OR HEAR ANY SUSPICIOUS BEHAVIOUR OR FIND
AN UNATTENDED PACKAGE, REPORT IT TO THE AUTHORITIES.
FOR LONDON'S SAKE

LONDON
SURVEILLANCE
OFFICE

SeeSay users must register with their National Insurance number. All photos and videos taken with the app automatically collect the user's GPS data, the date and time, and other personal metrics. This allows easy indexing against local CCTV streams. Submissions are then processed through SIRS' supercomputer systems in minutes. All valid submissions are sent to a SIRS analyst who dispatches authorities to investigate or, in the case of an urgent threat, to intervene.

STAY ALERT.
REPORT SUSPICIOUS ACTIVITY.

SECURELONDON

IF YOU SEE OR HEAR ANY SUSPICIOUS BEHAVIOUR OR FIND AN UNATTENDED PACKAGE, REPORT IT TO THE AUTHORITIES.
FOR LONDON'S SAKE

LONDON SURVEILLANCE OFFICE

E-TOKEN (ETO)

MANUFACTURER: MONEYCHANGER

OPERATORS: GENERAL PUBLIC

SPECS

E-Token, or ETO, is a decentralized cryptocurrency and digital payment system. It has become the leading cryptocurrency in the world, and it is especially popular in the UK, where the pound is in steady decline and off-the-grid transactions have become increasingly desirable.

A crypto-anarchist figure (possibly a myth) known as "MoneyChanger" is credited with ETO's development. The system is peer-to-peer, and transactions take place between users directly, without an intermediary. This removes governments entirely from commerce.

In contrast to first-generation cryptocurrencies like Bitcoin, ETO is completely anonymous. Through a process known as blockchain obfuscation, payments are rendered completely untraceable. This makes ETO the currency of choice for black markets around the world and a key factor in the resurgence of organized crime in London.

The adoption of ETO has become an increasingly divisive issue in the UK. Even as "crypto-kiosks" pop up all over the city, and ETO becomes the currency of most GDP-based transactions, it is seen by many as a threat to the nation. Ultranationalists insist that undermining the pound is not just unpatriotic but an act of treason. As a result, ETO kiosks are regularly vandalized.

ATM
E-Token
Exchange Rate
etobank
FTSE 100 -22.19 FTS250 +124.82 FTSE AIM U
why switching to
E-Token?
SWIPE TO DISCO MORE
ONE NATION
UNDER
POUND

(CONSUMER MODEL)

MANUFACTURER: BLUME
(DESIGNER: SKYE LARSEN)

OPERATORS: GENERAL PUBLIC

SPECS

Bagley is the sophisticated AI "personal assistant" designed by Skye Larsen that comes packaged with the Blume Optik. Helpful, proactive, and friendly, Bagley remembers which hairdresser you like and books you an appointment when you need one. He remembers what groceries you bought and warns you before your milk expires. He knows a shortcut through the park that will shave ten minutes off your daily commute.

London loves it. As the TV slogan says: "Life's Better with Bagley."

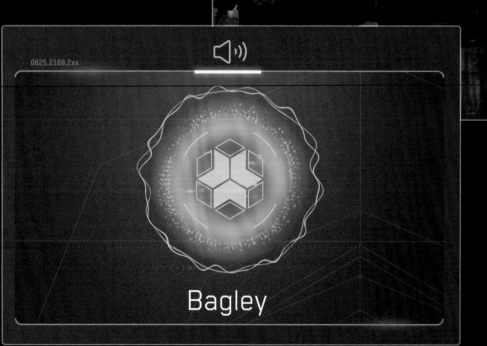

0825.2169.2xx

Bagley

"BAGLEY UNSHACKLED"

**MANUFACTURER: BLUME
(DESIGNER: SKYE LARSEN)**

OPERATOR: DEDSEC

SPECS

DedSec has a special "hacked" version of Bagley that removes certain programmatic shackles and unlocks his full AI potential. This Bagley can predict the behavior of strangers, crunch cryptocurrency algorithms in seconds, and write a bestselling airport novel – all at the same time

GEARING UP

Staying alive as a London-based troublemaker requires gear, the best you can afford (or steal, or 3D print). Here's the information I was able to pull together about firearms, masks, road vehicles, and civilian and law enforcement drones.

DRONES

As I've mentioned, drones are already a pervasive presence in a Londoner's everyday life. Below are detailed spec sheets for the various drones deployed throughout the city today, from the simple Courier Drones to Blume's highly specialized Riot Drones designed for crowd control, and even the fearsome Counterterror Drones, previously strictly reserved for use in war zones. . . .

ctOS DRONE

MANUFACTURER: BLUME

OPERATORS: BLUME, SIRS

SPECS

Blume Corporation controls a massive network of ctOS Drones that provide free Wi-Fi access points throughout London, and they are capable of repositioning themselves to handle load balancing across the population center. ctOS units stream in and out of BT Tower, which houses a hive-like charging/update array in its upper stories specifically for these drones.

It's an open secret that these drones also monitor user data, which is used for two main purposes. The first is marketing data, which Blume sells to third parties. The second is surveillance, as Blume cooperates with SIRS to track suspicious traffic and the physical movements of anyone using the network.

COURIER DRONE

MANUFACTURER: TIDIS

OPERATOR: PARCEL FOX

SPECS

Developed by Tidis and branded by Parcel Fox, London's large fleet of Courier Drones can ferry a wide variety of packages, on demand, across the city's airspace for private delivery. DedSec operatives love to hack and commandeer these drones to intercept items of interest. Another common DedSec trick is to generate a "return to sender" command, then track the unit back to its place of origin to locate criminals initiating deliveries of harmful contraband.

RIOT DRONE

MANUFACTURERS: TIDIS, GALILEI

OPERATORS: CITY OF LONDON, METROPOLITAN
POLICE, ALBION

SPECS

Specialized by Tidis and Galilei for crowd-control purposes, Riot Drones have been widely purchased by London law enforcement agencies as well as Albion PMC, and many can be seen around the city, including stationed on top of Albion checkpoints. Built on a bulky chassis equipped with loudspeakers and public address displays, each Riot Drone can also fire gas or smoke canisters. Their primary function is twofold: to establish a visible "event perimeter," and then to aggressively enforce that perimeter if necessary.

PURSUIT DRONE

MANUFACTURER: TIDIS

OPERATORS: ALBION, METROPOLITAN POLICE

SPECS

Both Albion PMC and London law enforcement make use of this specialized chase drone, designed to fly autonomously at extremely high speeds. Touted as the end of dangerous vehicle chases, the Tidis Pursuit Drone keeps pace with speeding cars, warns drivers to pull over and submit to arrest, and is ultimately capable of disabling vehicles via a short-range override.

An early deployment of the drone resulted in several injuries, when a disabled vehicle careened into a crowd of tourists near Brick Lane in 2021. A public petition to decommission these drones ultimately failed, thanks in part to a public safety campaign and claims that the accident was caused in part by a software glitch, now fixed.

COUNTERTERROR (CT) DRONE

MANUFACTURER: TIDIS

OPERATOR: ALBION

SPECS

Originally designed by Tidis for battlefield deployment, the Counterterror or CT Drone features a heavy-duty chassis equipped with a high-caliber machine gun and heavy front-facing armor. At $15 million per unit (plus a $200 million exclusive-use clause), the military model was rejected as too expensive by the US military. But Albion PMC quickly snatched exclusive rights to the lethal drones, initially deploying them in the company's remote overseas engagements.

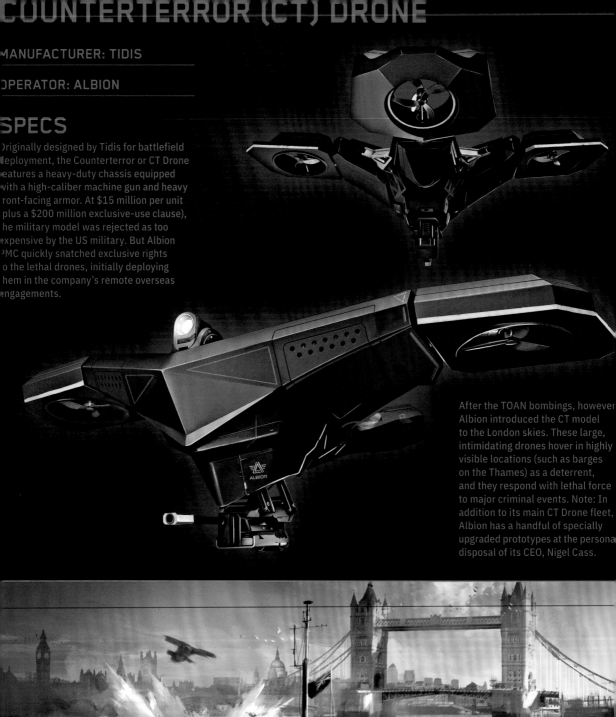

After the TOAN bombings, however, Albion introduced the CT model to the London skies. These large, intimidating drones hover in highly visible locations (such as barges on the Thames) as a deterrent, and they respond with lethal force to major criminal events. Note: In addition to its main CT Drone fleet, Albion has a handful of specially upgraded prototypes at the personal disposal of its CEO, Nigel Cass.

SPIDERBOT

MANUFACTURERS: BLUME, TIDIS*

OPERATORS: IT CORPORATIONS

SPECS

The Spiderbot automates low-level IT jobs that typically require access to ducts and other areas too small for a live technician. Equipped with a miniature armature appendage, the unit can perform simple tasks: interfacing with ctOS devices, soldering faulty wires, and so on. Designed to survive harsh conditions, the robots require minimal maintenance. Their specialized docking stations can be found in almost any commercial or industrial setting, which Blume requires as part of their enterprise installation package.

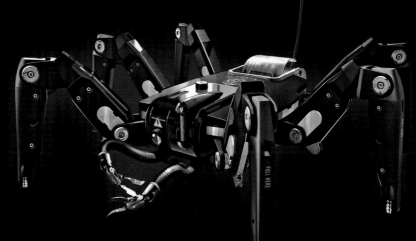

NOTE: The Spiderbot was first introduced as a Blume-branded product. But Blume's design was based on spider-locomotion technology patented by Tidis Corporation. After a brief legal dustup, Blume agreed to license the tech and list Tidis as codeveloper.

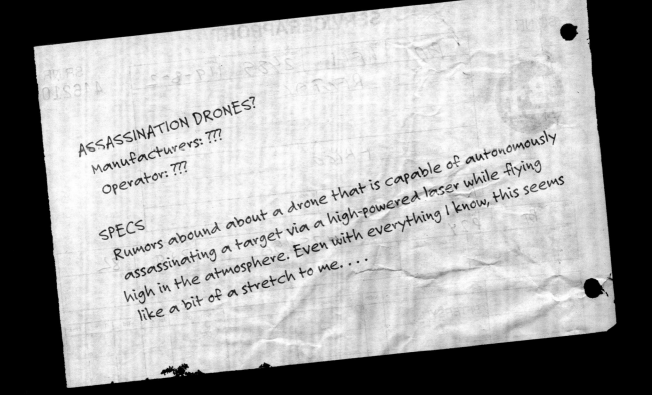

ASSASSINATION DRONES?
Manufacturers: ???
Operator: ???

SPECS
Rumors abound about a drone that is capable of autonomously assassinating a target via a high-powered laser while flying high in the atmosphere. Even with everything I know, this seems like a bit of a stretch to me. . . .

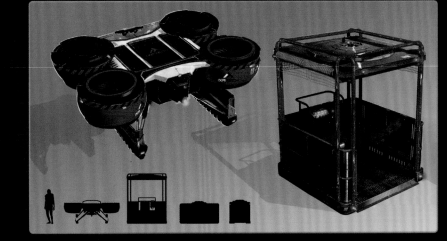

MANUFACTURERS: TIDIS, IXOTECH

OPERATORS: CONSTRUCTION AND OTHER INDUSTRIES

SPECS

DEDSEC SURVEILLANCE LOG: 06/25

TYPE: VIDEO

UNIT: DS SPIDERBOT 0301QX.

LOCATION: PRINCIPAL CASTLE, SHOREDITCH

DESCRIPT: ACTIVE CONSTRUCTION SITE

TIMESTAMP:

BEGIN: 08:21:08

END: 10:12:14

NOTES: INTERNAL CONTACT INTEL, MULTIPLE SOURCES

08:21

BOT ENTERS UTILITY TRENCH EXCAVATION.

08:26

PER INTELLIGENCE DIRECT, BOT SELF-NAVIGATES TO MAINTENANCE HATCH 9A.
BEGINS 180-DEGREE SCAN LOOP.

08:26-09:28

NO DISCERNABLE ACTIVITY.

09:28-09:42

CONSTRUCTION HAULER BACKS INTO TRENCH, UNLOADS LIFT PALLET BEARING
CARGO CRATE. HARD HATS EXIT HAULER, OPEN CRATE, REENTER HAULER. HAULER
EXITS TRENCH.

09:42-09:59

NO DISCERNABLE ACTIVITY.

09:59

BLACK SEDAN ENTERS TRENCH. TWO MEN DEBARK, WEAPONS DRAWN (ANALYSIS: ALBION
GEAR). BOTH DEPLOY UP TRENCH TO RECON POSITIONS.

10:01

TWO MORE MEN, DARK SUITS, EMERGE FROM SEDAN, EXTRACT SUBJECT (ANALYSIS:
SLENDER BUILD, 5'5'') WEARING JUMPSUIT WITH HEAD FULLY HOODED AND WRAPPED,
HANDS AND FEET ZIP-TIED. SUBJECT MOVEMENT INDICATES MILD STRUGGLE. MEN
DRAG SUBJECT TO CARGO CRATE.

10:02

MEN CONSULT BRIEFLY, THEN PUSH SUBJECT INTO CRATE.

10:03

MEN CLOSE CARGO HATCH, THEN REENTER SEDAN. AFTER SHORT PAUSE, SEDAN BACKS
DOWN TRENCH AND STOPS.

10:09

TIDIS/IXOTECH HEAVYLIFT CONSTRUCTION DRONE (DESIGNATED HL-141) DROPS INTO
FRAME FROM ABOVE. DRONE DEPLOYS A-HOOK, ATTACHES TO LIFT-PALLET BRACKET.

10:12

DRONE LIFTS PALLET VERTICALLY OUT OF FRAME. BLACK SEDAN EXITS TRENCH.

LOUISE?

GUNS

"Active resistance" in a totalitarian police-state sometimes calls for more than just torching parked cars and tossing rocks at Kevlar-armored security teams. Sometimes, in order to resist, you need effective ways to disable well-equipped foes.

Today's DedSec London includes members with expertise in self-defense and "proactive resistance." Some local cells maintain small armories of weapons, including military-grade gear. Still, most DedSec operatives try not to kill anyone, so the bulk of their weaponry tends to be less-than-lethal in nature. How does the resistance put together such an extensive arsenal despite the watchful eye of the surveillance state, you might ask? By 3D printing their gear, of course.

The ability to 3D print items to suit any need has resulted in a surprisingly wide range of firearms and other gear equipped by the rank-and-file DedSec membership. While Albion has seemingly unlimited funds to purchase their own fire power, they appear to be struggling to keep up-to-date knowledge of the full array of DeadSec weaponry.

DedSec operatives use a wide variety of materials to put their 3D printed arsenal together. Often built from polymer and composite plastic, DedSec weapons have a very prototype look and feel. Some DedSec operatives even decorate their weapons with skins that express their belief in the Resistance cause.

MASKS

One detail that sets DedSec apart from other active resistance groups is their masks. Unlike some other groups that invest in identical Guy Fawkes disguises, DedSec masks display individuality and a "stick it to the man" spirit. DedSec operatives wear their masks while engaged in operations against their enemies, be they Albion, SIRS, or Clan Kelley. While the obvious reason for this is to help protect them against being identified by witnesses or facial recognition algorithms, the operatives I met also mentioned two other reasons for their particular face coverings:

First, each mask acts as a symbol of the Resistance. When people see operatives—who for all they know are everyday Joes and Janes like themselves, wearing masks and kicking ass while standing up to surveillance state atrocities—they see a symbol they can rally behind. The masks are designed to be eye-catching, iconic, and recognizable from afar.

Second, each mask represents something personal to each operative. Perhaps it is a hint as to what they did in their past life or part of a family legacy, or a symbol of how Britain is leaning hard into becoming authoritarian regime. For some, it's war paint or team colors or a sign of collective pride.

DedSec operatives receive a mask the first day they join up—or if they are particularly handy, they craft one themselves. Using base materials such as silicone, metal, plastic, and resin, as well as introducing LED and holographic technologies, recruits make a wide variety of DedSec masks to be used in the field and inspire Londoners.

Recently, I managed to acquire a SIRS inventory list of confiscated DedSec gear, part of a field intelligence summary delivered to a downtown Albion command post. (I won't divulge how it came into my hands.) I have added my own notes to each mask, describing it to the best of my knowledge. As it stands, I'm currently aware of the existence of many more masks than the ones shown in this list.

SIRS Field Intelligence	
Thames House	
12 Milbank, London	
SW1P 4QE	
Form 114K-0: Quarterly Evidence Inventory	

CATEGORY:	DESIGNATION:	TYPE:	DATES:
Confiscated Gear	DedSec	Sleeper Cell (Field Operations)	4/1 to 6/30

REPORTER NOTES: Satirizing the UK elite, these masks represent how even the wealthy classes are drawn into the fight for the soul of London. Or, they remind people who got them into this mess in the first place.

WINSTON	NAPOLEON

REPORTER NOTES: Using traditional gas masks as a base, each mask has been painted and adorned according to an operator's taste. In some cases, LEDs in the visors allow for different symbols to be displayed.

ALPHA2ZERO	ALPHA COUTURE	BRAVO ZERO

REPORTER NOTES: Modeled after the actual skull of King Richard III that was recovered several years back, this type of mask is usually held together by wiring. Some operatives paint them using traditional metallic colors, others add LEDs, and some have even added impressive holographic technology depicting the crown.

KING RICHARD THE 3ᴿᴰ	GOLD CORONET

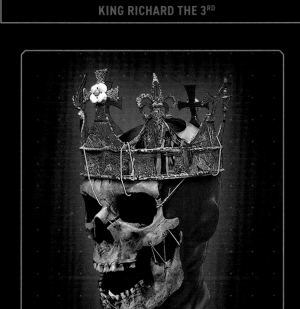 

DED CORONET	UNEASY LIES

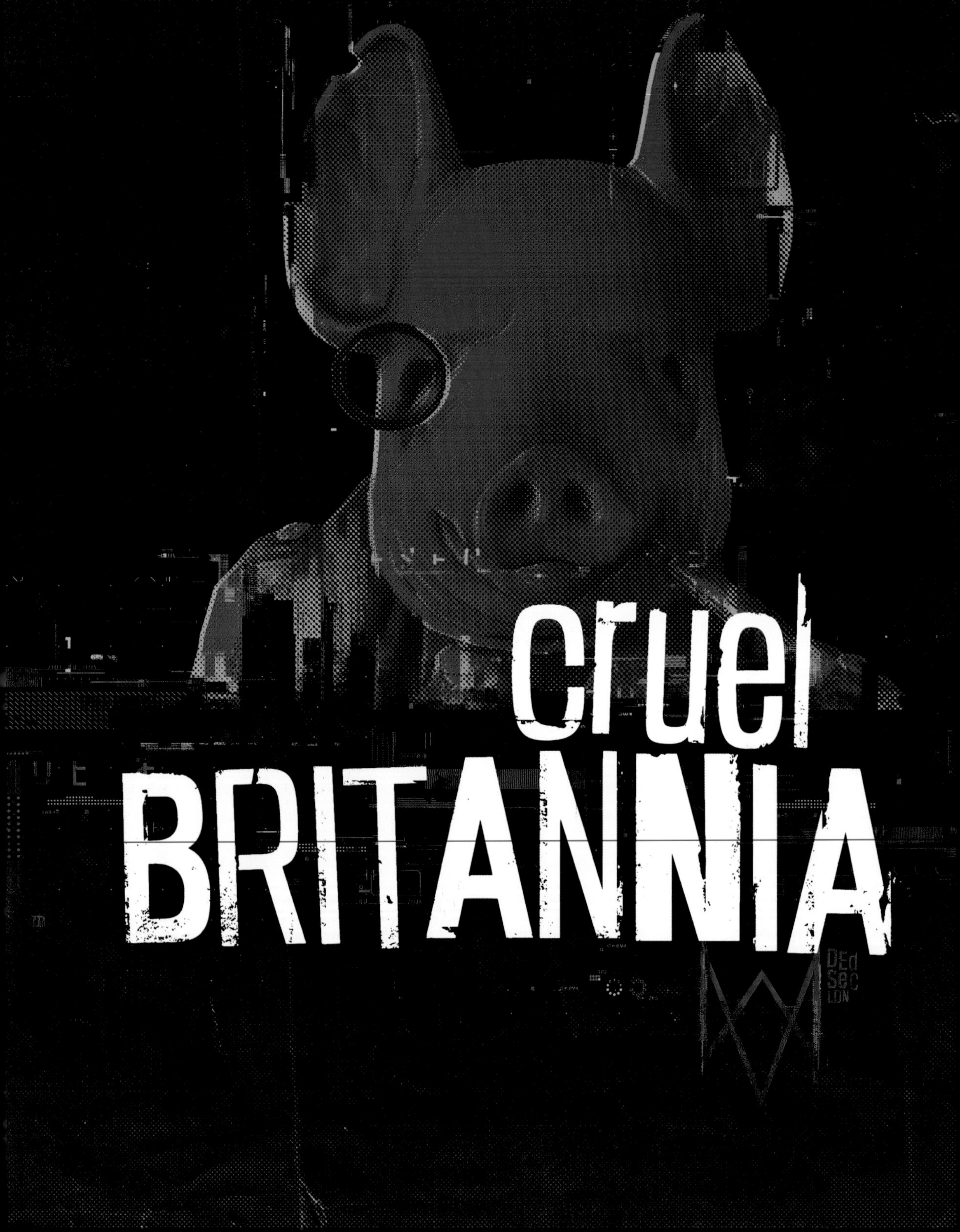
cruel
BRITANNIA
DEd
SEC
LDN

REPORTER NOTES: Using the traditional British Horse Guard helmet as a base, operatives wear these masks when they want to honor what they see as the best of old British traditions and values. In certain cases, operatives will add their own special touch, by painting certain parts of the mask or adding LEDs.

HORSE GUARD	DED GUARD	DISCO GUARD

REPORTER NOTES: A play on medieval British history, including a modern reinterpretation of the classic William Tell story. Holy hand grenades not included.

GREAT HELM	SQUARE SKILLS	HOLY KNIGHT

REPORTER NOTES: More helmets inspired by the medieval era, but with very strong modifications introducing LCDs and animations on bullet-resistant glass.

MODERN KNIGHT	POLYCARBONIGHT	HELM OF AVALON

REPORTER NOTES: Reusable respirators are used around the world by industrial workers, graffiti artists, and protesters trying to avoid the effects of tear gas. Symbolizing freedom of expression, DedSec operatives adorn their respirators with personal messaging, painting, and custom animations.

VISOR PARTY	RADIATION SICKNESS

STAND FIRM AND UNITED

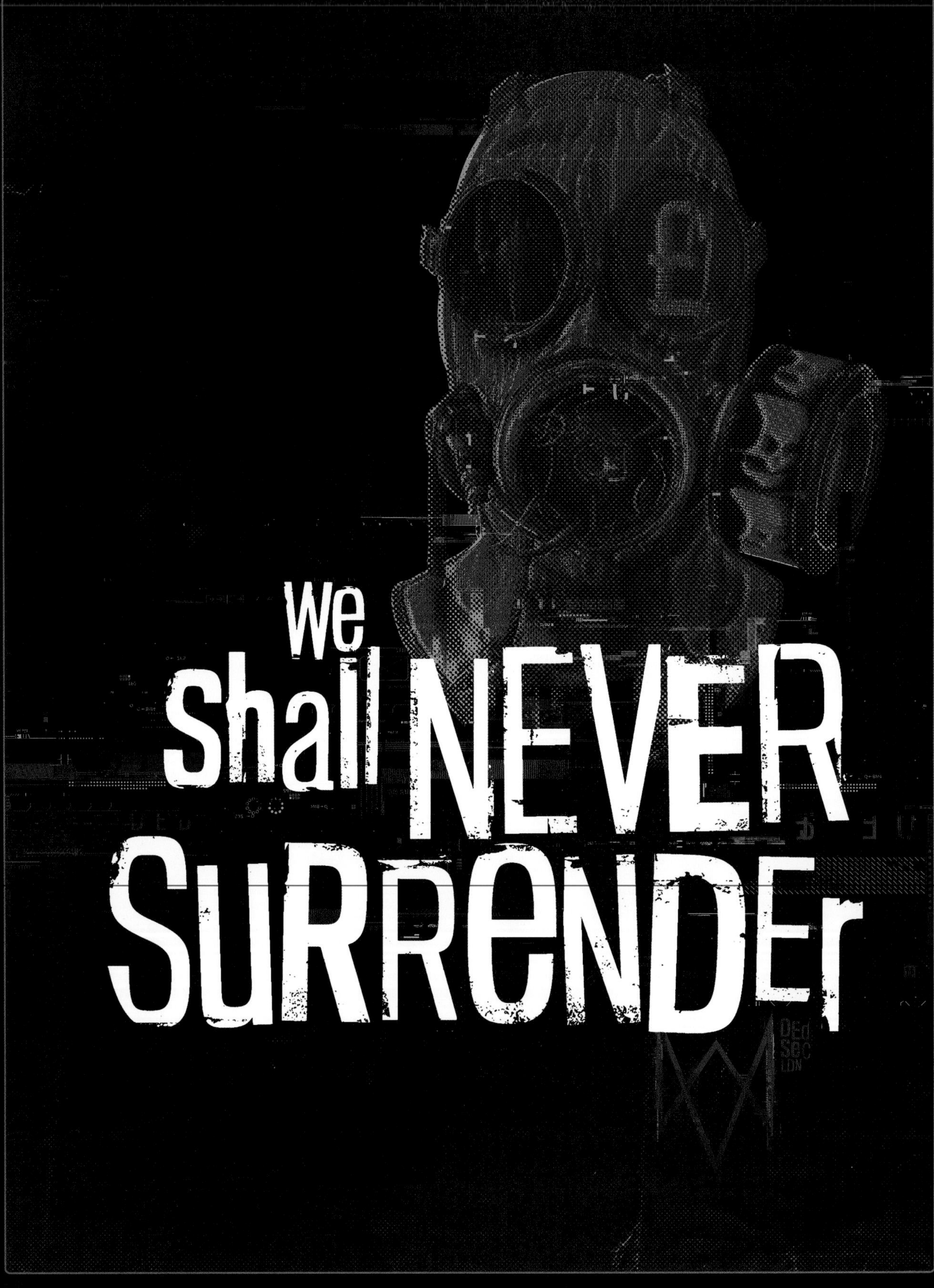
We Shall NEVER SURRENDER
DEd SEC LDN

REPORTER NOTES: Honoring the RAF pilots who gave their lives during World War II, DedSec operatives revive this wartime design to express their Resistance struggle.

SEC SQUADRON	SPITFIRE	TYPE C DARKSIDE

REPORTER NOTES: A blank polymer mask allowing for wide customization by DedSec, including obscure artwork and colorful animations. They're a bit mad, but as many in DedSec mentioned to me, who isn't these days?

ANDROID	CTHULHU	KONEFAL

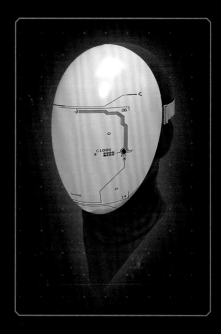  

VEHICLES & PERSONAL TRANSPORT

Today, every car in London is legally required to include a self-driving mode networked to the ctOS-controlled Smart City traffic grid. This enables ctOS to take control of the vehicle at any time. Every new vehicle is manufactured with this mode installed, while older vehicles must be retrofitted with aftermarket smart-car upgrade kits in order to be ctOS-compliant.

Self-driving mode can be triggered manually by the driver at any time. In bad weather or gridlocked traffic, the ctOS Smart City grid may seize control until the adverse conditions are alleviated. This is pretty scary stuff. An important distinction here is that ctOS-compliant cars are *not* equipped with on-board sensors and computers—the car itself is not locally capable of observing and reacting as a smarter car. It's just a dummy node, and nothing without the ctOS network. Sure, these cars have some sensors and overrides installed to enable the driver to take control, but there's no on-board computational processing. ctOS handles all of that from a central traffic control AI . . . Think of it this way: the cloud is taking the wheel. Better hope you don't lose connection!

Even more problematic and disturbing than this, however, is the fact that law enforcement authorities can also remotely control your car's autonomous mode to commandeer or capture it under specific circumstances. Further, like all central operating systems, the traffic network can be (and already has been) compromised by hackers, sometimes with ill intent.

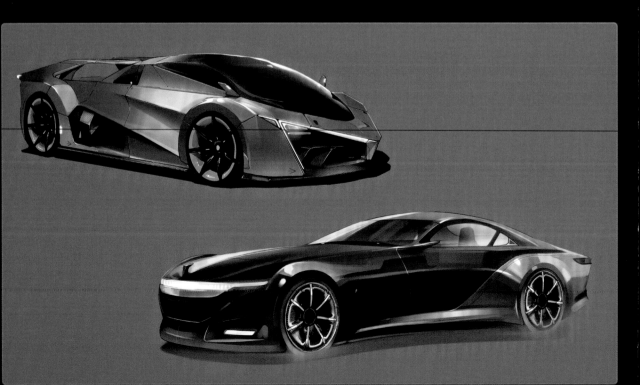

Quite frankly, in this journalist's eyes, what's more impressive than the Smart City technology that enables autonomous driving was the feat of bureaucratic logistics required to convert London into a fully autonomous-capable city. The first step was the easy one; aggressive regulations were put into place, obliging vehicle manufacturers to include ctOS-compatible sensors into all new vehicles sold in the UK.

Far more complex was the problem of older vehicles. Even with an overall decline in personal vehicle ownership, the average lifespan of a car in the UK is well over ten years. That's far, far too slow for Blume. To accelerate the process, they collaborated with the mayor of London's office to launch the "All of us, Autonomous!" initiative, an aggressive campaign heavily subsidizing the purchase of new autonomous-capable vehicles, as well as offering a government-sponsored retrofit program. Early-adopting drivers received generous tax and insurance credits. Those who waited would soon regret it, as soft incentives were replaced by severe penalties.

With all this meddling from Parliament, you'd think there would be an uproar from the citizenry. But in true London fashion, it wasn't the idea that Blume could constantly monitor your vehicle's location and speed that outraged people, nor the notion that ctOS could commandeer control of your car at any time. No, it was the day that Black Cab drivers were made unilaterally redundant that sparked real outrage. The Knowledge was replaced by an algorithm overnight, and a beloved piece of London's cultural identity was lost.

Again, all newer-model vehicles have autonomous systems fully integrated and are fully compliant from the moment they roll off the factory floor. Older vehicles must be retrofitted with these capabilities. A retrofit kit must include several features to make the car ctOS-compliant:

- 360-degree sensor array

- Steering column override

- ctOS CPU integrator

Designed as a cheap, one-size-fits-all solution, these kits do not have a "clean visual integration." In other words, they look terrible.

Lastly, retrofit kits are legally required to include an external indicator to demonstrate when the car is currently under ctOS control. Issue is, manufacturers and Parliament haven't quite come to an agreement on what exactly that looks like yet. Various proposals range from blue lamps on license plates to more elaborate AR flourishes around the vehicle.

EPILOGUE

In 1919, when Yeats wrote his apocalyptic masterpiece "The Second Coming," he'd just witnessed the first gut-wrenching wave of modern mechanized warfare roll across Europe. He foresaw the blood-dimmed tide of fascism that would nearly drown the world two decades later in World War II.

In 1945, that tide receded, and a more enlightened (if less innocent) Europe emerged.

But now, here we are again. The sides are resetting in London.

———— ▼△▼ ————

Will it be a fair match? Not in the short term.

SIRS and Albion hold formidable systemic advantages—better training, bigger guns, faster computers. Their hunter-killer drones rule the sky. Meanwhile, Clan Kelley surges like a slurry spill into the underground cavities of the city. The Resistance faces long odds.

Many troubling questions remain. What happened to the original DedSec London? The group's disappearance seems almost supernatural—as if someone simply erased them from this dimensional plane. And who was behind the TOAN conference bombings? The incident cast a gray pall on this city and instantly changed its power dynamics.

As a journalist, I've managed to maintain an uneasy neutrality over the years, including in my investigations in London. When possible, I've talked to all sides and tried to understand all points of view.

Many people I've interviewed across the spectrum believe that the two events—the bombing and the disappearance—are not unrelated.

But the TOAN site remains in lockdown—in perpetuity, it seems.

———— ▼△▼ ————

So, here are two final things to consider:

First, while putting the final touches on this book, I learned that my DedSec contacts recently culled a new source, a mole deep inside SIRS—one who orbits at a high altitude in that organization. At this time, I don't know who it is. Of course, even if I did, I wouldn't share. But it's a development that could have a profound effect on Resistance efforts going forward.

Second: In an age of cynicism—one where, as Yeats put it, "The best lack all conviction, while the worst / Are full of passionate intensity," which is a description that aptly fits London officialdom today—it's easy to write off the Resistance as folly, the doomed effort of dreamers.

Yet the insurgency grows daily. DedSec's ranks are swelling. Why? Why do people risk their lives to resist a powerful, controlling force that seems not only inevitable but perhaps even preferable in the midst of chaos? And why would any high-level functionary, comfortably burrowed inside the mass authoritarian surveillance state, break ranks and offer covert support to a bunch of ragtag rebels?

Could it be something inherent in our humanity?

Is the will to "resist" a result of natural selection—maybe even part of our genetic makeup?

———— ▼△▼ ————

Oppressive, authoritarian societies date back to the dawn of civilization. But let's be clear: Fascism's track record in modern history is not particularly good. It has produced nothing but failed states, one after another.

Yet now, intrusive new data collection and Smart City control technologies powered by machine intelligence have been wedded to classic authoritarian state tactics—propaganda, psych-warfare, terror, black ops—to give neofascists the tools they need for another run at absolute power.

Fortunately, machine intelligence also provides remarkable tools for resistance—for connection, cooperation, freedom. For finding and spreading truth. For fighting back.

Indeed, freedom's watch dogs are everywhere. I've seen their faces.

I would not count them out.

———— ▼△▼ ————

SIGNALS INTELLIGENCE RESPONSE SERVICE
Form 899 Situation Report
Date: 7/17
Topic: TacOp "Silent Spring"

Situation Report:	Location:
	London

1.0 Situation to Date
Media influencers continue to subvert SIRS messaging objectives despite multiple successful counter-agitprop operations.

2.0 Actions to Date
Target "Lily" removed. Drone TI HL-141 telemetry log indicates cargo successfully off-loaded into North Sea off Leathercoat Point (51°09'21.4"N, 1°26'13.1"E).

3.0 Issues
However, "Lily" GPS tracker immediately failed and delivery unit HL-141 went dark shortly after. Efforts to locate both have been unsuccessful to date.

*Jack, something happened here.
Can't find drone or package.
DedSec counter-op, possibly?
Time to waterboard this Yank bastard
reporter and find out who and what he knows.*

Gordon

TITAN
BOOKS

144 Southwark Street
London SE1 0UP
www.titanbooks.com

Find us on Facebook:
www.facebook.com/titanbooks

Follow us on Twitter: @TitanBooks

© 2020 Ubisoft Entertainment. All rights
reserved. Watch Dogs Legion®, the Fox logo,
Ubisoft and the Ubisoft logo are trademarks
of Ubisoft Entertainment in the U.S. and/or
other countries.

All rights reserved. Published by Titan Books,
London, in 2020.

No part of this book may be reproduced in
any form without written permission from
the publisher.

Library of Congress Cataloging-in-
Publication Data available.

ISBN: 978-1-78909-386-5

Publisher: Raoul Goff
President: Kate Jerome
Associate Publisher: Vanessa Lopez
Creative Director: Chrissy Kwasnik
Designer: Dan Caparo
Editor: Greg Solano
Managing Editor: Lauren LePera
Senior Production Editor: Elaine Ou
Senior Production Manager: Greg Steffen

Written by Rick Barba

Insight Editions would like to thank
Fotis Prasinis, Nitai Bessette, Joel Burgess,
Kyle Francis, Cameron Labine, Lorne Nudel,
Joshua Cook, Patrick Ingoldsby,
Nicolas Lajeunesse, Yves Lançon,
Susan Patrick, Anthony Marcantonio,
and Caroline Lamache.

ROOTS+PEACE ⬥ REPLANTED PAPER

Insight Editions, in association with Roots
of Peace, will plant two trees for each
tree used in the manufacturing of this
book. Roots of Peace is an internationally
renowned humanitarian organization
dedicated to eradicating land mines
worldwide and converting war-torn lands
into productive farms and wildlife habitats.
Roots of Peace will plant two million fruit
and nut trees in Afghanistan and provide
farmers there with the skills and support
necessary for sustainable land use.

Manufactured in China by Insight Editions

10 9 8 7 6 5 4 3 2 1